中华人民共和国公司法

Company Law of the People's Republic of China

(中英对照)
(Chinese-English)

法 律 出 版 社
Law Press China

中华人民共和国主席令

第二十九号

《全国人民代表大会常务委员会关于修改〈中华人民共和国公司法〉的决定》已由中华人民共和国第九届全国人民代表大会常务委员会第十三次会议于1999年12月25日通过,现予公布,修改后的《中华人民共和国公司法》和本决定自公布之日起施行。

中华人民共和国主席 江泽民
1999年12月25日

Order of the President of the People's Republic of China

No. 29

The Decision of the Standing Committee of the National People's Congress on Revising the Company Law of the People's Republic of China, adopted at the 13th Meeting of the Standing Committee of the Ninth National People's Congress of the People's Republic of China on December 25, 1999, is hereby promulgated, and the revised Company Law of the People's Republic of China and this Decision shall go into effect as of the date of promulgation.

Jiang Zemin
President of the People's Republic of China
December 25, 1999

全国人民代表大会常务委员会关于修改《中华人民共和国公司法》的决定

(1999年12月25日第九届全国人民代表大会常务委员会第十三次会议通过)

第九届全国人民代表大会常务委员会第十三次会议审议了国务院关于《中华人民共和国公司法修正案(草案)》的议案,决定对《中华人民共和国公司法》作如下修改:

一、第六十七条修改为:"国有独资公司监事会主要由国务院或者国务院授权的机构、部门委派的人员组成,并有公司职工代表参加。监事会的成员不得少于三人。监事会行使本法第五十四条第一款第(一)、(二)项规定的职权和国务院规定的其他职权。""监事列席董事会会议。""董事、经理及财务负责人不得兼任监事。"

二、第二百二十九条增加一款作为第二款:"属于高新技术的股份有限公司,发起人以工业产权和非专利技术作

Decision of the Standing Committee of the National People's Congress on Revising the Company Law of the People's Republic of China

(Adopted at the 13th Meeting of the Standing Committee of the Ninth National People's Congress on December 25, 1999)

At its 13th Meeting, the Standing Committee of the Ninth National People's Congress, upon deliberation of the Draft Amendment to the Company Law of the People's Republic of China proposed by the State Council, decides to make the following revisions of the Company Law of the People's Republic of China:

1. Article 67 is revised as follows: "The supervisory board of a wholly State-owned Company shall be mainly composed of members appointed by the State Council or by the institutions or departments authorized by the State Council, and shall include representatives of the staff and workers of the company. The component members of the supervisory board shall be no less than three persons. The supervisory board shall exercise the functions and powers specified in subparagraphs (1) and (2) of the first paragraph of Article 54 of this Law and other functions and powers specified by the State Council."

"The supervisors shall attend meetings of the board of directors as non-

价出资的金额占公司注册资本的比例,公司发行新股、申请股票上市的条件,由国务院另行规定。"

《中华人民共和国公司法》根据本决定作相应的修改,重新公布。

支持有条件的高新技术股份有限公司进入证券市场直接融资,有利于高新技术产业发展。对高新技术的股份有限公司运用资本市场筹集发展资金,要坚持国家产业政策,符合高新技术要求。根据高新技术股份有限公司的特点,其上市交易的股票在现有的证券交易所内单独组织交易系统,进行交易。鉴于此项工作还缺乏经验,加之风险较大,应当有计划、有步骤、积极稳妥地进行。

本决定自公布之日起施行。

voting participants.""Directors, the manager and persons in charge of financial affairs of the company may not concurrently serve as supervisors."

2. One paragraph is added as the second paragraph of Article 229: "With regard to a new and high-tech joint stock limited company, the proportion of the investment, made by a promoter in the form of industrial property rights and non-patent technology at their appraised value, in the registered capital of the company, the requirements the company must meet in order to issue new shares or apply to have the shares listed shall be separately formulated by the State Council."

The Company Law of the People's Republic of China shall be revised correspondingly according to this Decision and promulgated anew.

It is favourable for the development of new and high-tech industries to support new and high-tech joint stock limited companies, where conditions permit, in their efforts to enter the share market for direct financing. Any new and high-tech joint stock limited company that wishes to make use of the capital market to raise development funds shall adhere to the industrial policies of the State and meet the requirements for high and new technology. In view of the characteristics of the new and high-tech joint stock limited companies, a separate network shall be established in the existing stock exchanges for the trading of listed shares of such companies. Due to lack of experience in this field of work, not to mention the considerable risks involved, the work should be done enthusiastically, steadily, systematically and in a well-planned way.

This Decision shall go into force as of the date of its promulgation.

中华人民共和国公司法

(1993年12月29日第八届全国人民代表大会常务委员会第五次会议通过根据1999年12月25日第九届全国人民代表大会常务委员会第十三次会议《关于修改〈中华人民共和国公司法〉的决定》修正)

目 录

第一章 总 则
第二章 有限责任公司的设立和组织机构
 第一节 设 立
 第二节 组织机构
 第三节 国有独资公司
第三章 股份有限公司的设立和组织机构
 第一节 设 立
 第二节 股东大会
 第三节 董事会、经理
 第四节 监事会
第四章 股份有限公司的股份发行和转让

Company Law of the People's Republic of China

(Adopted at the Fifth Meeting of the Standing Committee of the Eighth National People's Congress on December 29, 1993 and revised at the 13th Meeting of the Ninth National People's Congress on December 25, 1999 in accordance with the Decision on Revising the Company Law of the People's Republic of China)

Contents

Chapter I　General Provisions
Chapter II　Incorporation and Organizational Structure of Limited Liability Companies
　Section 1　Incorporation
　Section 2　Organizational Structure
　Section 3　Wholly State-owned Companies
Chapter III　Incorporation and Organizational Structure of Joint Stock Limited Companies
　Section 1　Incorporation
　Section 2　Shareholders General Meetings
　Section 3　Board of Directors and Manager
　Section 4　Supervisory Board
Chapter IV　Issue and Transfer of Shares of Joint Stock Limited

第一节　股份发行

第二节　股份转让

第三节　上市公司

第五章　公司债券

第六章　公司财务、会计

第七章　公司合并、分立

第八章　公司破产、解散和清算

第九章　外国公司的分支机构

第十章　法律责任

第十一章　附则

第一章　总　　则

第一条　为了适应建立现代企业制度的需要,规范公司的组织和行为,保护公司、股东和债权人的合法权益,维护社会经济秩序,促进社会主义市场经济的发展,根据宪法,制定本法。

第二条　本法所称公司是指依照本法在中国境内设立的有限责任公司和股份有限公司。

第三条　有限责任公司和股份有限公司是企业法人。

有限责任公司,股东以其出资额为限对公司承担责任,

                Companies
- Section 1   Issue of Shares
- Section 2   Transfer of Shares
- Section 3   Listed Companies
- Chapter V   Company Bonds
- Chapter VI   Financial Affairs and Accounting of Companies
- Chapter VII   Merger and Division of Companies
- Chapter VIII   Bankruptcy, Dissolution and Liquidation of Companies
- Chapter IX   Branches of Foreign Companies
- Chapter X   Legal Liability
- Chapter XI   Supplementary Provisions

Chapter I   General Provisions

Article 1   This Law is formulated in accordance with the Constitution of the People's Republic of China in order to meet the needs of establishing a modern enterprise system, to standardize the organization and activities of companies, to protect the legitimate rights and interests of companies, shareholders and creditors, to maintain socio-economic order and to promote the development of the socialist market economy.

Article 2   The term "company" mentioned in this Law refers to a limited liability company or a joint stock limited company incorporated within the territory of the People's Republic of China in accordance with this Law.

Article 3   A "limited liability company" or "joint stock limited company" is an enterprise legal person.

In the case of a limited liability company, shareholders shall assume liability towards the company to the extent of their respective

公司以其全部资产对公司的债务承担责任。

股份有限公司,其全部资本分为等额股份,股东以其所持股份为限对公司承担责任,公司以其全部资产对公司的债务承担责任。

第四条 公司股东作为出资者按投入公司的资本额享有所有者的资产受益、重大决策和选择管理者等权利。

公司享有由股东投资形成的全部法人财产权,依法享有民事权利,承担民事责任。

公司中的国有资产所有权属于国家。

第五条 公司以其全部法人财产,依法自主经营,自负盈亏。

公司在国家宏观调控下,按照市场需求自主组织生产经营,以提高经济效益、劳动生产率和实现资产保值增值为目的。

第六条 公司实行权责分明、管理科学、激励和约束相结合的内部管理体制。

第七条 国有企业改建为公司,必须依照法律、行政法规规定的条件和要求,转换经营机制,有步骤地清产核资,

capital contributions, and the company shall be liable for its debts to the extent of all its assets.

In the case of a joint stock limited company, its total capital shall be divided into equal shares, shareholders shall assume liability towards the company to the extent of their respective shareholdings, and the company shall be liable for its debts to the extent of all its assets.

Article 4 The shareholders of a company shall, in their capacity of contributors of capital, enjoy such rights of owners as benefitting from assets of the company, making major decisions and selecting managerial personnel in accordance with the amount of their respective capital investment in the company.

A company shall enjoy the right to the entire property of the legal person formed by the investments of the shareholders and shall possess civil rights and bear the civil liabilities in accordance with the law.

The ownership of State-owned assets in a company shall vest in the State.

Article 5 A company shall, with all its legal person assets, operate independently and be responsible for its own profits and losses according to law.

A company shall, under the macro-adjustment and control of the State, organize its production and operation independently in accordance with market demand for the purpose of raising economic benefits and labour productivity and maintaining and increasing the value of its assets.

Article 6 An internal management mechanism shall be implemented within companies, which is characterized by clear definition of powers and responsibilities, scientific management and combination of encouragement and restraint.

Article 7 State-owned enterprises restructured to form companies must transform their operating mechanism, gradually produce an

界定产权,清理债权债务,评估资产,建立规范的内部管理机构。

第八条 设立有限责任公司、股份有限公司,必须符合本法规定的条件。符合本法规定的条件的,登记为有限责任公司或者股份有限公司;不符合本法规定的条件的,不得登记为有限责任公司或者股份有限公司。

法律、行政法规对设立公司规定必须报经审批的,在公司登记前依法办理审批手续。

第九条 依照本法设立的有限责任公司,必须在公司名称中标明有限责任公司字样。

依照本法设立的股份有限公司,必须在公司名称中标明股份有限公司字样。

第十条 公司以其主要办事机构所在地为住所。

第十一条 设立公司必须依照本法制定公司章程。公司章程对公司、股东、董事、监事、经理具有约束力。

公司的经营范围由公司章程规定,并依法登记。公司的经营范围中属于法律、行政法规限制的项目,应当依法经

inventory of their assets and verify their funds, delimit their property rights, clear off their claims and debts, evaluate their assets and establish a standard internal management mechanism in accordance with the conditions and requirements set by laws, administrative rules and regulations.

Article 8 Incorporation of limited liability companies or joint stock limited companies must meet the conditions stipulated by the present Law. Companies meeting the conditions set by this Law shall be registered as limited liability companies or joint stock limited companies; while companies failing to meet the conditions set by this Law shall not be registered as limited liability companies or joint stock limited companies.

Where laws or administrative rules and regulations provide that incorporation of companies must be subject to examination and approval, the procedures of examination and approval shall be completed according to law prior to the registration of such companies.

Article 9 A limited liability company established according to this Law must clearly indicate the words "limited liability company" in its name.

A joint stock limited company established according to this Law must clearly indicate the words "joint stock limited company" in its name.

Article 10 A company's domicile shall be the place where its main administrative organization is located.

Article 11 Articles of association must be formulated in accordance with this Law when a company is incorporated. A company's articles of association shall have binding force on the company, its shareholders, directors, supervisors and managers.

A company's scope of business shall be defined in its articles of association and registered in accordance with the law. Items within the

过批准。

公司应当在登记的经营范围内从事经营活动。公司依照法定程序修改公司章程并经公司登记机关变更登记,可以变更其经营范围。

第十二条 公司可以向其他有限责任公司、股份有限公司投资,并以该出资额为限对所投资公司承担责任。

公司向其他有限责任公司、股份有限公司投资的,除国务院规定的投资公司和控股公司外,所累计投资额不得超过本公司净资产的百分之五十,在投资后,接受被投资公司以利润转增的资本,其增加额不包括在内。

第十三条 公司可以设立分公司,分公司不具有企业法人资格,其民事责任由公司承担。

公司可以设立子公司,子公司具有企业法人资格,依法独立承担民事责任。

第十四条 公司从事经营活动,必须遵守法律,遵守职业道德,加强社会主义精神文明建设,接受政府和社会公众的监督。

公司的合法权益受法律保护,不受侵犯。

company's "scope of business" that are subject to restrictions under laws, administrative rules and regulations shall be approved in accordance with the law.

Companies shall engage in business activities within their registered scope of business. A company may change its scope of business by amending its articles of association in accordance with statutory procedures and making such amendments registered with the Company Registration Authority.

Article 12 A company may invest in other limited liability companies or joint stock limited companies and shall assume liability towards the company so invested in to the extent of such capital contributions.

In case a company, other than an investment company or a holding company as specified by the State Council, invests in other limited liability companies or joint stock limited companies, the aggregated amount of such investments shall not exceed fifty percent of its net assets; after the initial investment, the increase therein resulting from capitalization of the profit derived from the company invested in shall not be included.

Article 13 A company may establish branches, which shall not possess the status of enterprise legal persons and whose civil liabilities shall be borne by the company.

A company may establish subsidiaries, which shall possess the status of enterprise legal persons, and shall independently bear civil liabilities according to law.

Article 14 A company must, when engaging in business activities, abide by the law, observe professional ethics, strengthen the construction of socialist culture and ideology and accept supervision of the government and the public.

The legitimate rights and interests of companies shall be protected

第十五条　公司必须保护职工的合法权益,加强劳动保护,实现安全生产。

　　公司采用多种形式,加强公司职工的职业教育和岗位培训,提高职工素质。

　　第十六条　公司职工依法组织工会,开展工会活动,维护职工的合法权益。公司应当为本公司工会提供必要的活动条件。

　　国有独资公司和两个以上的国有企业或者其他两个以上的国有投资主体投资设立的有限责任公司,依照宪法和有关法律的规定,通过职工代表大会和其他形式,实行民主管理。

　　第十七条　公司中中国共产党基层组织的活动,依照中国共产党章程办理。

　　第十八条　外商投资的有限责任公司适用本法,有关中外合资经营企业、中外合作经营企业、外资企业的法律另有规定的,适用其规定。

by the law and shall be inviolable.

Article 15 Companies must protect the lawful rights and interests of their staff and workers, and strengthen labour protection so as to achieve safety in production.

Companies shall apply various forms to strengthen professional education and on-the-job training of their staff and workers so as to improve their quality.

Article 16 Company's staff and workers shall, in accordance with the law, organize a trade union to carry out the trade union activities and protect the lawful rights and interests of the staff and workers. The company shall provide its trade union with conditions necessary for carrying out its activities.

Wholly State-owned companies and limited liability companies invested in and established by two or more State-owned enterprises or by two or more other State-owned investment entities shall, through staff and workers congresses or other forms, practise democratic management in accordance with the provisions of the Constitution and relevant laws.

Article 17 The grass-root organizations of the Communist Party of China in companies shall carry out their activities in accordance with the Constitution of the Communist Party of China.

Article 18 The present Law shall apply to limited liability companies with foreign investment. Where laws concerning Chinese-foreign equity joint ventures, Chinese-foreign contractual joint ventures and foreign-funded enterprises provides otherwise, such provisions shall prevail.

第二章 有限责任公司的设立和组织机构

第一节 设 立

第十九条 设立有限责任公司,应当具备下列条件:

(一)股东符合法定人数;

(二)股东出资达到法定资本最低限额;

(三)股东共同制定公司章程;

(四)有公司名称,建立符合有限责任公司要求的组织机构;

(五)有固定的生产经营场所和必要的生产经营条件。

第二十条 有限责任公司由二个以上五十个以下股东共同出资设立。

国家授权投资的机构或者国家授权的部门可以单独投资设立国有独资的有限责任公司。

第二十一条 本法施行前已设立的国有企业,符合本法规定设立有限责任公司条件的,单一投资主体的,可以依

Chapter II Incorporation and Organizational Structure of Limited Liability Companies

Section 1 Incorporation

Article 19 The following conditions must be fulfilled for the incorporation of a limited liability company:

(1) the number of shareholders conforms to the statutory number;

(2) the capital contributions of the shareholders reach the statutory minimum amount of capital;

(3) the shareholders have jointly formulated the articles of association of the company;

(4) the company has a name and an organizational structure established in compliance with the requirements for a limited liability company; and

(5) there are fixed premises and necessary conditions for production and operation.

Article 20 A limited liability company shall be jointly invested in and incorporated by not less than two and not more than fifty shareholders.

State-authorized investment institutions or departments authorized by the State may independently invest in and establish wholly State-owned limited liability companies.

Article 21 If State-owned enterprises established prior to the implementation of this Law comply with the conditions stipulated in this Law for the incorporation of limited liability companies, they may, in the case of enterprises with a single investing entity, be

照本法改建为国有独资的有限责任公司；多个投资主体的，可以改建为前条第一款规定的有限责任公司。

国有企业改建为公司的实施步骤和具体办法，由国务院另行规定。

第二十二条 有限责任公司章程应当载明下列事项：

（一）公司名称和住所；

（二）公司经营范围；

（三）公司注册资本；

（四）股东的姓名或者名称；

（五）股东的权利和义务；

（六）股东的出资方式和出资额；

（七）股东转让出资的条件；

（八）公司的机构及其产生办法、职权、议事规则；

（九）公司的法定代表人；

（十）公司的解散事由与清算办法；

（十一）股东认为需要规定的其他事项。

股东应当在公司章程上签名、盖章。

第二十三条 有限责任公司的注册资本为在公司登记

restructured as wholly State-owned limited liability companies in accordance with this Law, or in the case of enterprises with multiple investing entities, be restructured as limited liability companies as specified in the first paragraph of the preceding Article.

The implementation procedures and specific measures for restructuring State-owned enterprises as companies shall be formulated separately by the State Council.

Article 22 The articles of association of limited liability companies shall specify the following particulars:

(1) the name and domicile of the company;

(2) the scope of business of the company;

(3) the registered capital of the company;

(4) the names or titles of the shareholders;

(5) the rights and obligations of the shareholders;

(6) the method and amount of capital contributions by the shareholders;

(7) the conditions for transfer of capital contributions by shareholders;

(8) the organization of the company, its method of creation, functions and powers and the rules of procedure;

(9) the legal representative of the company;

(10) the reasons for dissolution of the company and method of liquidation; and

(11) other items which the shareholders deem necessary to be specified.

The shareholders shall sign and affix their seals to the company's articles of association.

Article 23 The registered capital of a limited liability company shall be the amount of the paid-up capital contributions of all its shareholders as registered with the Company Registration Authority.

机关登记的全体股东实缴的出资额。

有限责任公司的注册资本不得少于下列最低限额：

（一）以生产经营为主的公司人民币五十万元；

（二）以商品批发为主的公司人民币五十万元；

（三）以商业零售为主的公司人民币三十万元；

（四）科技开发、咨询、服务性公司人民币十万元。

特定行业的有限责任公司注册资本最低限额需高于前款所定限额的，由法律、行政法规另行规定。

第二十四条 股东可以用货币出资，也可以用实物、工业产权、非专利技术、土地使用权作价出资。对作为出资的实物、工业产权、非专利技术或者土地使用权，必须进行评估作价，核实财产，不得高估或者低估作价。土地使用权的评估作价，依照法律、行政法规的规定办理。

以工业产权、非专利技术作价出资的金额不得超过有限责任公司注册资本的百分之二十，国家对采用高新技术成果有特别规定的除外。

第二十五条 股东应当足额缴纳公司章程中规定的各自所认缴的出资额。股东以货币出资的，应当将货币出资

The registered capital of a limited liability company shall be no less than the following minima:

(1) RMB 500,000 yuan for a company engaged mainly in production and operation;

(2) RMB 500,000 yuan for a company engaged mainly in commodity wholesale;

(3) RMB 300,000 yuan for a company engaged mainly in commercial retailing; and

(4) RMB 100,000 yuan for a company engaged in science and technology development, consultancy or services.

Where the minimum registered capital of a limited liability company in specified trades needs to be higher than those stipulated in the preceding paragraph, it shall be stipulated by the laws and administrative rules and regulations separately.

Article 24 A shareholder may make its capital contributions to a company in currency or by contributing material objects, industrial property rights, non-patented technology and land-use rights at their appraised value. The material objects, industrial property rights, non-patented technology or land-use rights to be contributed as capital must undergo an asset valuation and verification, and shall not be overvalued or undervalued. The appraisal and valuation of land-use rights shall be handled in accordance with the laws and administrative rules and regulations.

The investment in the form of industrial property rights and non-patented technology at their appraised value shall not exceed twenty percent of the registered capital of a limited liability company, except where special State regulations in respect of the application of high and new technological achievement provide otherwise.

Article 25 Each shareholder shall make in full the amount of the capital contribution subscribed for under the articles of association of

足额存入准备设立的有限责任公司在银行开设的临时帐户；以实物、工业产权、非专利技术或者土地使用权出资的，应当依法办理其财产权的转移手续。

股东不按照前款规定缴纳所认缴的出资，应当向已足额缴纳出资的股东承担违约责任。

第二十六条　股东全部缴纳出资后，必须经法定的验资机构验资并出具证明。

第二十七条　股东的全部出资经法定的验资机构验资后，由全体股东指定的代表或者共同委托的代理人向公司登记机关申请设立登记，提交公司登记申请书、公司章程、验资证明等文件。

法律、行政法规规定需要经有关部门审批的，应当在申请设立登记时提交批准文件。

公司登记机关对符合本法规定条件的，予以登记，发给公司营业执照；对不符合本法规定条件的，不予登记。

the company. Where a shareholder makes its capital contribution in currency, it shall deposit the full amount of such capital contribution in currency in the interim bank account opened by the limited liability company to be established. Where a shareholder makes its capital contribution in the form of material objects, industrial property rights, non-patented technology or land-use rights, the transfer procedures for the property rights shall be handled in accordance with the law.

Shareholders failing to make the capital contributions they subscribed for in accordance with the preceding paragraph shall be liable for breach of contract towards the shareholders who have made in full their capital contributions.

Article 26 After all shareholders have made their capital contributions in full, such contributions must be verified by a statutory capital verification institution which shall issue capital verification certificates.

Article 27 After the total capital contributions of the shareholders have been verified by a statutory capital verification institution, application shall be made to the Company Registration Authority for registration of the incorporation of the company by a representative designated by all the shareholders or by an agent jointly entrusted by them, who shall submit such documents as an application for registration, the articles of association and the capital verification certificate.

Where the examination and approval of the relevant authorities is required by the laws or administrative rules and regulations, the approval documents shall be submitted on application for registration of incorporation.

The Company Registration Authority shall grant registration and issue a business licence to a company that meets the requirements stipulated in this Law; the Company Registration Authority shall not register a company failing to meet the requirements stipulated in this Law.

公司营业执照签发日期,为有限责任公司成立日期。

第二十八条　有限责任公司成立后,发现作为出资的实物、工业产权、非专利技术、土地使用权的实际价额显著低于公司章程所定价额的,应当由交付该出资的股东补交其差额,公司设立时的其他股东对其承担连带责任。

第二十九条　设立有限责任公司的同时设立分公司的,应当就所设分公司向公司登记机关申请登记,领取营业执照。

有限责任公司成立后设立分公司,应当由公司法定代表人向公司登记机关申请登记,领取营业执照。

第三十条　有限责任公司成立后,应当向股东签发出资证明书。

出资证明书应当载明下列事项:

(一)公司名称;

(二)公司登记日期;

(三)公司注册资本;

(四)股东的姓名或者名称、缴纳的出资额和出资日期;

(五)出资证明书的编号和核发日期。

The date of the issuance of the company business license shall be the date of the incorporation of a limited liability company.

Article 28 Where, after the incorporation of a limited liability company, it is discovered that the actual value of the material objects, industrial property rights, non-patented technology or land-use rights contributed as capital is notably less than the value stated in the articles of association, the shareholders that made such contributions shall make up the discrepancy. Those who are shareholders at the time of the incorporation of the company shall bear joint and several liability therefor.

Article 29 Where branches are established simultaneously with the incorporation of a limited liability company, application for registration of the branches established shall be made to, and business licences shall be obtained from, the Company Registration Authority.

Where a limited liability company establishes branches after its incorporation, the company's legal representative shall apply for the registration to, and obtain business licences from, the Company Registration Authority.

Article 30 After a limited liability company has been incorporated, it shall issue capital contribution certificates to its shareholders.

A capital contribution certificate shall specify the following items:

(1) the name of the company;

(2) the registration date of the company;

(3) the registered capital of the company;

(4) the name or title of the shareholder, the amount and date of its capital contribution; and

(5) the serial number of the capital contribution certificate and the date of its verification and issuance.

出资证明书由公司盖章。

第三十一条 有限责任公司应当置备股东名册,记载下列事项:

(一)股东的姓名或者名称及住所;

(二)股东的出资额;

(三)出资证明书编号。

第三十二条 股东有权查阅股东会会议记录和公司财务会计报告。

第三十三条 股东按照出资比例分取红利。公司新增资本时,股东可以优先认缴出资。

第三十四条 股东在公司登记后,不得抽回出资。

第三十五条 股东之间可以相互转让其全部出资或者部分出资。

股东向股东以外的人转让其出资时,必须经全体股东过半数同意;不同意转让的股东应当购买该转让的出资,如果不购买该转让的出资,视为同意转让。

经股东同意转让的出资,在同等条件下,其他股东对该出资有优先购买权。

第三十六条 股东依法转让其出资后,由公司将受让人的姓名或者名称、住所以及受让的出资额记载于股东名册。

A capital contribution certificate shall bear the seal of the company on it.

Article 31 A limited liability company shall prepare a roster of its shareholders with the following items therein:

(1) the names or titles and domiciles of the shareholders;

(2) the amounts of capital contributions of the shareholders; and

(3) the serial numbers of the capital contribution certificates.

Article 32 A shareholder shall have the right to look up the minutes of shareholders meetings and the financial and accounting reports of the company.

Article 33 Shareholders shall draw dividends in proportion to their capital contributions. Where a company increases capital, the existing shareholders shall have priority in subscription for new shares.

Article 34 Once a company is registered, its shareholders may not withdraw their capital contributions.

Article 35 The shareholders of a company may assign among themselves all or part of their capital contributions.

Where a shareholder intends to assign its capital contribution to persons who are not shareholders, the consent of over half of all the shareholders must be secured. Those shareholders disapproving the assignment shall purchase the capital contribution to be assigned. If such shareholders do not make the purchase, they shall be deemed to have consented to the assignment.

Other shareholders shall, under identical terms, have priority in purchasing the capital contribution to be assigned with the consent of the shareholders.

Article 36 After a shareholder has assigned its capital contribution according to law, the company shall record the name or title and domicile of the consignee and the amount of the capital contribution assigned in the roster of the shareholders.

第二节 组织机构

第三十七条 有限责任公司股东会由全体股东组成,股东会是公司的权力机构,依照本法行使职权。

第三十八条 股东会行使下列职权:

(一)决定公司的经营方针和投资计划;

(二)选举和更换董事,决定有关董事的报酬事项;

(三)选举和更换由股东代表出任的监事,决定有关监事的报酬事项;

(四)审议批准董事会的报告;

(五)审议批准监事会或者监事的报告;

(六)审议批准公司的年度财务预算方案、决算方案;

(七)审议批准公司的利润分配方案和弥补亏损方案;

(八)对公司增加或者减少注册资本作出决议;

(九)对发行公司债券作出决议;

(十)对股东向股东以外的人转让出资作出决议;

(十一)对公司合并、分立、变更公司形式、解散和清算等事项作出决议;

(十二)修改公司章程。

Section 2 Organizational Structure

Article 37 The shareholders meeting of a limited liability company shall be composed of all the shareholders. The shareholders meeting shall be the organ of power of the company and shall exercise its functions and powers in accordance with this Law.

Article 38 The shareholders meeting shall exercise the following functions and powers:

(1) to decide on the business policy and investment plan of the company;

(2) to elect and recall members of the board of directors and to decide on matters concerning the remuneration of directors;

(3) to elect and recall supervisors appointed from among the shareholders representatives, and to decide on matters concerning the remuneration of supervisors;

(4) to examine and approve reports of the board of directors;

(5) to examine and approve reports of the supervisory board or supervisors;

(6) to examine and approve the annual financial budget plan and final accounts plan of the company;

(7) to examine and approve plans for profit distribution of the company and plans for making up losses;

(8) to adopt resolutions on the increase or reduction of the registered capital of the company;

(9) to adopt resolutions on the issuance of company bonds;

(10) to adopt resolutions on the assignment of capital contribution by a shareholder to a person other than the shareholders;

(11) to adopt resolutions on matters such as the merger, division, transformation, dissolution and liquidation of the company; and

第三十九条　股东会的议事方式和表决程序,除本法有规定的以外,由公司章程规定。

股东会对公司增加或者减少注册资本、分立、合并、解散或者变更公司形式作出决议,必须经代表三分之二以上表决权的股东通过。

第四十条　公司可以修改章程。修改公司章程的决议,必须经代表三分之二以上表决权的股东通过。

第四十一条　股东会会议由股东按照出资比例行使表决权。

第四十二条　股东会的首次会议由出资最多的股东召集和主持,依照本法规定行使职权。

第四十三条　股东会会议分为定期会议和临时会议。

定期会议应当按照公司章程的规定按时召开。代表四分之一以上表决权的股东,三分之一以上董事,或者监事,可以提议召开临时会议。

有限责任公司设立董事会的,股东会会议由董事会召集,董事长主持,董事长因特殊原因不能履行职务时,由董

(12) to amend the articles of association of the company.

Article 39 The rules of deliberation and voting procedures of the shareholders meeting shall, except where provided for by this Law, be stipulated by the articles of association of the company.

Resolutions of the shareholders meeting on the increase or reduction of the registered capital, the division, merger, dissolution, or transformation of the company must be adopted by shareholders of the company representing two-thirds or more of the voting rights.

Article 40 A company may amend its articles of association. A resolution on the amendment to the articles of association must be adopted by shareholders of the company representing two-thirds or more of the voting rights.

Article 41 Shareholders shall exercise their voting rights at the shareholders' meeting in proportion to their capital contributions.

Article 42 The first meeting of the shareholders of a company shall be convened and presided over by the shareholder who has made the biggest capital contribution to the company and shall exercise its functions and powers in accordance with this Law.

Article 43 Shareholders meetings shall be divided into regular meetings and interim meetings.

Regular shareholders meetings shall be convened on time as stipulated by the articles of association of the company. Interim shareholders meetings may be convened upon proposal made by shareholders representing one-fourth or more of the voting rights, or, by one-third or more of directors or supervisors.

Where a limited liability company has set up a board of directors, its shareholders meetings shall be convened by the board of directors and presided over by the chairman of the board. Where special circumstances preclude the chairman of the board from performing his function, the meeting shall be presided over by a vice-chairman or a

事长指定的副董事长或者其他董事主持。

第四十四条 召开股东会会议,应当于会议召开十五日以前通知全体股东。

股东会应当对所议事项的决定作成会议记录,出席会议的股东应当在会议记录上签名。

第四十五条 有限责任公司设董事会,其成员为三人至十三人。

两个以上的国有企业或者其他两个以上的国有投资主体投资设立的有限责任公司,其董事会成员中应当有公司职工代表。董事会中的职工代表由公司职工民主选举产生。

董事会设董事长一人,可以设副董事长一至二人。董事长、副董事长的产生办法由公司章程规定。

董事长为公司的法定代表人。

第四十六条 董事会对股东会负责,行使下列职权:

(一)负责召集股东会,并向股东会报告工作;

(二)执行股东会的决议;

(三)决定公司的经营计划和投资方案;

(四)制订公司的年度财务预算方案、决算方案;

(五)制订公司的利润分配方案和弥补亏损方案;

director of the board designated by the chairman.

Article 44 All shareholders shall be notified fifteen days prior to the convening of a shareholders meeting.

The shareholders meeting shall keep minutes of their decisions on matters discussed at it; the shareholders present at the meeting shall sign the minutes.

Article 45 A limited liability company shall have a board of directors, which shall be composed of three to thirteen members.

The members of the board of directors of a limited liability company invested in and established by two or more State-owned enterprises, or by two or more other State-owned investment entities shall include representatives of the staff and workers of the company. Such representatives of the staff and workers shall be democratically elected by the staff and workers of the company.

A board of directors shall have a chairman and one or two vice-chairmen. The method for the creation of the chairman and vice-chairmen shall be stipulated in the articles of association of the company.

The chairman of the board of directors shall be the company's legal representative.

Article 46 The board of directors shall be responsible to the shareholders meeting, and exercise the following functions and powers:

(1) to be responsible for convening shareholders meetings and to report on its work to the shareholders meetings;

(2) to implement the resolutions of the shareholders meetings;

(3) to decide on the business plans and investment plans of the company;

(4) to formulate the annual financial budget plan and final accounts plan of the company;

(5) to formulate plans for profit distribution and plans for making

(六)制订公司增加或者减少注册资本的方案;

(七)拟订公司合并、分立、变更公司形式、解散的方案;

(八)决定公司内部管理机构的设置;

(九)聘任或者解聘公司经理(总经理)(以下简称经理),根据经理的提名,聘任或者解聘公司副经理、财务负责人,决定其报酬事项;

(十)制定公司的基本管理制度。

第四十七条 董事任期由公司章程规定,但每届任期不得超过三年。董事任期届满,连选可以连任。

董事在任期届满前,股东会不得无故解除其职务。

第四十八条 董事会会议由董事长召集和主持;董事长因特殊原因不能履行职务时,由董事长指定副董事长或者其他董事召集和主持。三分之一以上董事可以提议召开董事会会议。

第四十九条 董事会的议事方式和表决程序,除本法

up losses of the company;

(6) to formulate plans for the increase or reduction of the registered capital of the company;

(7) to formulate plans for the merger, division, transformation and dissolution of the company;

(8) to decide on the establishment of the company's internal management organs;

(9) to appoint or dismiss the company's manager (general manager) (hereinafter referred to as "manager"), and, upon recommendation of the manager, to appoint and dismiss the company's deputy manager (s) and persons in charge of the financial affairs of the company, and to decide on matters concerning their remuneration; and

(10) to formulate the basic management system of the company.

Article 47 The term of office of directors shall be stipulated by the articles of association of the company but may not exceed three years. A director may, if reelected upon expiration of his term of office, serve consecutive terms.

The shareholders meeting of a company may not unwarrantedly dismiss a director of the board prior to the expiration of his term of office.

Article 48 Meetings of the board of directors shall be convened and presided over by the chairman of the board. Where special circumstances preclude the chairman from performing his function, the meeting shall be convened and presided over by a vice-chairman or a director of the board designated by the chairman. One-third or more of the members of the board of directors may propose the convening of a meeting of the board of directors.

Article 49 The rules of deliberation and voting procedures of the board of directors shall, except where provided for by this Law, be

有规定的以外,由公司章程规定。

召开董事会会议,应当于会议召开十日以前通知全体董事。

董事会应当对所议事项的决定作成会议记录,出席会议的董事应当在会议记录上签名。

第五十条 有限责任公司设经理,由董事会聘任或者解聘。经理对董事会负责,行使下列职权:

(一)主持公司的生产经营管理工作,组织实施董事会决议;

(二)组织实施公司年度经营计划和投资方案;

(三)拟订公司内部管理机构设置方案;

(四)拟订公司的基本管理制度;

(五)制定公司的具体规章;

(六)提请聘任或者解聘公司副经理、财务负责人;

(七)聘任或者解聘除应由董事会聘任或者解聘以外的负责管理人员;

(八)公司章程和董事会授予的其他职权。

经理列席董事会会议。

第五十一条 有限责任公司,股东人数较少和规模较

stipulated by the articles of association of the company.

All directors shall be notified ten days prior to the convening of a board meeting.

The board meeting shall keep minutes of decisions on matters discussed at it; directors present at the meeting shall sign the minutes.

Article 50 A limited liability company shall have a manager, who shall be appointed or dismissed by the board of directors. The manager shall be responsible to the board of directors and shall exercise the following functions and powers:

(1) to be in charge of the production, operation and management of the company, and to organize the implementation of the resolutions of the board of directors;

(2) to organize the implementation of the annual business plans and investment plans of the company;

(3) to draw up plans on the establishment of the internal management organs of the company;

(4) to draw up the basic management system of the company;

(5) to formulate specific rules and regulations of the company;

(6) to recommend the appointment or dismissal of the deputy manager(s) and of persons in charge of the financial affairs of the company;

(7) to appoint or dismiss management personnel other than those to be appointed or dismissed by the board of directors; and

(8) other functions and powers granted by the articles of association of the company and the board of directors.

The manager shall attend meetings of the board of directors as a non-voting attendant.

Article 51 Where a limited liability company has a small number of shareholders and is comparatively small in scale, it may have an executive director instead of a board of directors. The executive

小的,可以设一名执行董事,不设立董事会。执行董事可以兼任公司经理。

执行董事的职权,应当参照本法第四十六条规定,由公司章程规定。

有限责任公司不设董事会的,执行董事为公司的法定代表人。

第五十二条 有限责任公司,经营规模较大的,设立监事会,其成员不得少于三人。监事会应在其组成人员中推选一名召集人。

监事会由股东代表和适当比例的公司职工代表组成,具体比例由公司章程规定。监事会中的职工代表由公司职工民主选举产生。

有限责任公司,股东人数较少和规模较小的,可以设一至二名监事。

董事、经理及财务负责人不得兼任监事。

第五十三条 监事的任期每届为三年。监事任期届满,连选可以连任。

第五十四条 监事会或者监事行使下列职权:

(一)检查公司财务;

(二)对董事、经理执行公司职务时违反法律、法规或者公司章程的行为进行监督;

director may concurrently serve as the manager of the company.

The powers and functions of the executive director shall be stipulated by the articles of association of the company with reference to Article 46 of this Law.

Where a limited liability company does not have a board of directors, the executive director shall be the legal representative of the company.

Article 52 A limited liability company with a relatively large-scale business shall have a supervisory board composed of no less than three members. The supervisory board shall elect a convener from among its members.

The supervisory board shall be composed of representatives of the shareholders and an appropriate proportion of the staff and workers of the company. The exact proportion shall be stipulated in the articles of association. The representatives of the staff and workers in the supervisory board shall be democratically elected by the staff and workers of the company.

Where a limited liability company has a small number of shareholders and is comparatively small in scale, it may have one or two supervisors.

Directors, the manager or personnel in charge of financial affairs of the company may not concurrently serve as supervisors.

Article 53 The term of office of a supervisor shall be three years. A supervisor may, if reelected upon expiration of his term of office, serve consecutive terms.

Article 54 The supervisory board or the supervisors shall exercise the following functions and powers:

(1) to examine the financial affairs of the company;

(2) to supervise the acts of the directors and the manager violating the laws, administrative rules and regulations or the articles of association of the

(三)当董事和经理的行为损害公司的利益时,要求董事和经理予以纠正;

(四)提议召开临时股东会;

(五)公司章程规定的其他职权。

监事列席董事会会议。

第五十五条 公司研究决定有关职工工资、福利、安全生产以及劳动保护、劳动保险等涉及职工切身利益的问题,应当事先听取公司工会和职工的意见,并邀请工会或者职工代表列席有关会议。

第五十六条 公司研究决定生产经营的重大问题、制定重要的规章制度时,应当听取公司工会和职工的意见和建议。

第五十七条 有下列情形之一的,不得担任公司的董事、监事、经理:

(一)无民事行为能力或者限制民事行为能力;

(二)因犯有贪污、贿赂、侵占财产、挪用财产罪或者破坏社会经济秩序罪,被判处刑罚,执行期满未逾五年,或者

company during the performance of their functions;

(3) to demand directors and the manager to make corrections if any of their acts is found to have damaged the interests of the company;

(4) to propose the convening of interim shareholders meetings; and

(5) other functions and powers as stipulated in the articles of association of the company.

The supervisors shall attend meetings of the board of directors as non-voting participants.

Article 55 A company shall, in studying and deciding on issues involving the personal interests of its staff and workers such as their salaries, welfare, safety in production, labour protection and labour insurance, solicit in advance the opinions of the trade union and the staff and workers of the company. And representatives of the trade union or of the staff and workers shall be invited to attend relevant meetings as non-voting participants.

Article 56 A company shall solicit the opinions and suggestions of the trade union and the staff and workers of the company when studying and deciding on major issues concerning production and operation, and formulating important rules and regulations.

Article 57 None of the following persons may hold the position of director, supervisor or manager of a company:

(1) a person without capacity or with restricted capacity for civil acts;

(2) a person who was sentenced to criminal punishment for the crime of embezzlement, bribery, seizure of property or misappropriation of property or for undermining the socio-economic order, where not more than five years have elapsed since the expiration of the enforcement period; or a person who was deprived of his

因犯罪被剥夺政治权利,执行期满未逾五年;

(三)担任因经营不善破产清算的公司、企业的董事或者厂长、经理,并对该公司、企业的破产负有个人责任的,自该公司、企业破产清算完结之日起未逾三年;

(四)担任因违法被吊销营业执照的公司、企业的法定代表人,并负有个人责任的,自该公司、企业被吊销营业执照之日起未逾三年;

(五)个人所负数额较大的债务到期未清偿。

公司违反前款规定选举、委派董事、监事或者聘任经理的,该选举、委派或者聘任无效。

第五十八条 国家公务员不得兼任公司的董事、监事、经理。

第五十九条 董事、监事、经理应当遵守公司章程,忠实履行职务,维护公司利益,不得利用在公司的地位和职权为自己谋取私利。

董事、监事、经理不得利用职权收受贿赂或者其他非法收入,不得侵占公司的财产。

第六十条 董事、经理不得挪用公司资金或者将公司资金借贷给他人。

董事、经理不得将公司资产以其个人名义或者以其他个人名义开立帐户存储。

political rights for committing a crime, where not more than five years have elapsed since the expiration of the enforcement period;

(3) a director, or factory head or manager who was personally responsible for the bankruptcy liquidation of the company or enterprise due to mismanagement, where not more than three years have elapsed since the date of completion of the bankruptcy liquidation;

(4) a legal representative of the company or enterprise that had the business license revoked for violating the law, where such representative bear individual liability therefor and not more than three years have elapsed since the date of revocation of the business license; and

(5) a person with relatively large amount of personal debts that have fallen due but haven't been settled.

Where a company elects or appoints a director or supervisor or engages the manager in violation of the preceding paragraph, such election, appointment or engagement shall be invalid.

Article 58 Government functionaries may not concurrently serve as directors, supervisors or managers of companies.

Article 59 Directors, supervisors and the manager of a company shall comply with the articles of association of the company, faithfully perform their duties and maintain the interests of the company and shall not take advantage of their position, functions and powers in the company to seek personal gains.

Directors, supervisors and the manager of a company shall not, by taking advantage of their functions and powers, accept bribes or other unlawful incomes, nor may they misappropriate the property of the company.

Article 60 Directors and the manager of a company shall not misappropriate company funds or lend company funds to others.

Directors and the manager shall not deposit company assets in their own personal accounts or in personal accounts of other individuals.

董事、经理不得以公司资产为本公司的股东或者其他个人债务提供担保。

第六十一条 董事、经理不得自营或者为他人经营与其所任职公司同类的营业或者从事损害本公司利益的活动。从事上述营业或者活动的,所得收入应当归公司所有。

董事、经理除公司章程规定或者股东会同意外,不得同本公司订立合同或者进行交易。

第六十二条 董事、监事、经理除依照法律规定或者经股东会同意外,不得泄露公司秘密。

第六十三条 董事、监事、经理执行公司职务时违反法律、行政法规或者公司章程的规定,给公司造成损害的,应当承担赔偿责任。

第三节 国有独资公司

第六十四条 本法所称国有独资公司是指国家授权投资的机构或者国家授权的部门单独投资设立的有限责任公司。

国务院确定的生产特殊产品的公司或者属于特定行业的公司,应当采取国有独资公司形式。

第六十五条 国有独资公司的公司章程由国家授权投

Directors and the manager shall not use company assets as security for the personal debts of shareholders of the company or of other individuals.

Article 61 Directors and the manager shall not operate their own in, or operate for others, the same category of business as the company they are serving or, engage in activities which damage the interests of the company. If a director or the manager engages in such business or activities, the incomes derived therefrom shall belong to the company.

Directors and the manager shall not enter into contracts or conduct transactions with the company except as provided for in the articles of association or approved by the shareholders meeting.

Article 62 Directors, supervisors and the manager shall not disclose any company secrets except as provided for by the law or approved by the shareholders' meeting.

Article 63 Directors, supervisors and the manager shall be liable for compensation, if they violate the laws, administrative rules and regulations or the articles of association in performance of their duties and thus cause damage to the company.

Section 3 Wholly State-owned Companies

Article 64 A wholly State-owned company mentioned in this Law means a limited liability company invested in and established solely by the State-authorized investment institution or a department authorized by the State.

Companies which manufacture special products as determined by the State Council or companies that belong to the category of specialized trades shall adopt the form of wholly State-owned companies.

Article 65 The articles of association of a wholly State-owned company shall be formulated by the State-authorized investment

资的机构或者国家授权的部门依照本法制定,或者由董事会制订,报国家授权投资的机构或者国家授权的部门批准。

第六十六条　国有独资公司不设股东会,由国家授权投资的机构或者国家授权的部门,授权公司董事会行使股东会的部分职权,决定公司的重大事项,但公司的合并、分立、解散、增减资本和发行公司债券,必须由国家授权投资的机构或者国家授权的部门决定。

第六十七条　国有独资公司监事会主要由国务院或者国务院授权的机构、部门委派的人员组成,并有公司职工代表参加。监事会的成员不得少于三人。监事会行使本法第五十四条第一款第(一)、(二)项规定的职权和国务院规定的其他职权。

监事列席董事会会议。

董事、经理及财务负责人不得兼任监事。

第六十八条　国有独资公司设立董事会,依照本法第四十六条、第六十六条规定行使职权。董事会每届任期为三年。

institution or a department authorized by the State in accordance with this Law, or be formulated by the board of directors of the company and submitted for the approval of the relevant State-authorized investment institution or the department authorized by the State.

Article 66 A wholly State-owned company shall not have a shareholders meeting. The State-authorized investment institution or the department authorized by the State shall authorize the board of directors of the company to exercise part of the functions and powers of the shareholders meeting and to make decisions on important matters of the company. However, the merger, division, dissolution, increase and reduction of capital, and issuance of company bonds must be decided by the State-authorized investment institution or by the department authorized by the State.

Article 67 The supervisory board of a wholly State owned Company shall be mainly composed of members appointed by the State Council or by the institutions or departments authorized by the State Council, and shall include representatives of the staff and workers of the company. The component members of the supervisory board shall be no less than three persons. The supervisory board shall exercise the functions and powers specified in subparagraphs (1) and (2) of the first paragraph of Article 54 of this Law and other functions and powers specified by the State Council.

The supervisors shall attend meetings of the board of directors as non-voting participants.

Directors, the manager and persons in charge of financial affairs of the company may not concurrently serve as supervisors.

Article 68 A wholly State-owned company shall have a board of directors, which shall exercise its functions and powers in accordance with the provisions of Article 46 and Article 66 of this Law. Each term of office of directors shall be three years.

公司董事会成员为三人至九人，由国家授权投资的机构或者国家授权的部门按照董事会的任期委派或者更换。董事会成员中应当有公司职工代表。董事会中的职工代表由公司职工民主选举产生。

董事会设董事长一人，可以视需要设副董事长。董事长、副董事长，由国家授权投资的机构或者国家授权的部门从董事会成员中指定。

董事长为公司的法定代表人。

第六十九条　国有独资公司设经理，由董事会聘任或者解聘。经理依照本法第五十条规定行使职权。

经国家授权投资的机构或者国家授权的部门同意，董事会成员可以兼任经理。

第七十条　国有独资公司的董事长、副董事长、董事、经理，未经国家授权投资的机构或者国家授权的部门同意，不得兼任其他有限责任公司、股份有限公司或者其他经营组织的负责人。

第七十一条　国有独资公司的资产转让，依照法律、行政法规的规定，由国家授权投资的机构或者国家授权的部

The board of directors shall be composed of three to nine members, who shall be appointed and replaced by the State-authorized investment institution or by the department authorized by the State in accordance with the term of office of the board of directors. The board of directors shall include representatives of the staff and workers of the company. The representatives of the staff and workers on the board of directors shall be democratically elected by the staff and workers of the company.

The board of directors shall have a chairman and may have a vice-chairman, if necessary. The chairman and vice-chairman shall be designated by the State-authorized investment institution or the department authorized by the State from among members of the board of directors.

The chairman of the board of directors shall be the legal representative of the company.

Article 69 A wholly State-owned company shall have a manager, who shall be engaged and dismissed by the board of directors. The manager shall exercise his functions and powers in accordance with the provisions of Article 50 of this Law.

A member of the board of directors may, subject to the consent of the State-authorized investment institution or the department authorized by the State, serve concurrently as manager.

Article 70 The chairman, vice-chairman and directors of the board, or the manager of a wholly State-owned company may not, without the consent of the State-authorized investment institution or the department authorized by the State, serve concurrently as responsible persons in other limited liability companies, joint-stock limited companies or other business organizations.

Article 71 Where a wholly State-owned company transfers its assets, the procedures for examination and approval, and the transfer

门办理审批和财产权转移手续。

第七十二条 经营管理制度健全、经营状况较好的大型的国有独资公司,可以由国务院授权行使资产所有者的权利。

第三章 股份有限公司的设立和组织机构

第一节 设 立

第七十三条 设立股份有限公司,应当具备下列条件:

(一)发起人符合法定人数;

(二)发起人认缴和社会公开募集的股本达到法定资本最低限额;

(三)股份发行、筹办事项符合法律规定;

(四)发起人制订公司章程,并经创立大会通过;

(五)有公司名称,建立符合股份有限公司要求的组织机构;

(六)有固定的生产经营场所和必要的生产经营条件。

of property rights shall be handled by the State-authorized investment institution or the department authorized by the State in accordance with the laws and administrative rules and regulations.

Article 72 Large-sized wholly State-owned companies with a sound business management system and relatively successful operations may be authorized by the State Council to exercise the rights of asset owners.

Chapter III Incorporation and Organizational Structure of Joint Stock Limited Companies

Section 1 Incorporation

Article 73 To incorporate a joint stock limited company, the following conditions must be satisfied:

(1) the number of sponsors shall conform to the statutory number;

(2) the share capital subscribed for by the sponsors and raised from the general public shall reach the statutory minimum amount of capital;

(3) the issuance of shares and preparations for incorporation shall be in conformity with the provisions of the law;

(4) the articles of association of the company shall be formulated by the sponsors and adopted at the inaugural meeting;

(5) the company shall have a name and an organizational structure required for the incorporation of a joint stock limited company; and

(6) the company shall have fixed premises and the necessary conditions for production and operation.

第七十四条　股份有限公司的设立,可以采取发起设立或者募集设立的方式。

发起设立,是指由发起人认购公司应发行的全部股份而设立公司。

募集设立,是指由发起人认购公司应发行股份的一部分,其余部分向社会公开募集而设立公司。

第七十五条　设立股份有限公司,应当有五人以上为发起人,其中须有过半数的发起人在中国境内有住所。

国有企业改建为股份有限公司的,发起人可以少于五人,但应当采取募集设立方式。

第七十六条　股份有限公司发起人,必须按照本法规定认购其应认购的股份,并承担公司筹办事务。

第七十七条　股份有限公司的设立,必须经过国务院授权的部门或者省级人民政府批准。

第七十八条　股份有限公司的注册资本为在公司登记机关登记的实收股本总额。

股份有限公司注册资本的最低限额为人民币一千万元。股份有限公司注册资本最低限额需高于上述所定限额的,由法律、行政法规另行规定。

Article 74 Joint stock limited companies may be by means of sponsorship or by means of share offer.

Incorporation by means of sponsorship means incorporation of a company by means of subscription by the sponsors for all the shares to be issued by the company.

Incorporation by means of share offer means incorporation of a company by means of subscription by the sponsors for a portion of the shares to be issued by the company and offer of the rest to the general public.

Article 75 To incorporate a joint stock limited company, there shall be five or more sponsors, of which more than half must have their domicile within the territory of the People's Republic of China.

Where a State-owned enterprise is restructured as a joint stock limited company, there may be less than five sponsors, however, such a company shall be incorporated by means of share offer.

Article 76 The sponsors of a joint stock limited company must subscribe in accordance with this Law for the shares to be subscribed for by them, and shall undertake the matters concerning the preparation for the incorporation of the company.

Article 77 The incorporation of a joint stock limited company must be subject to the approval of a department authorized by the State Council or of a people's government at the provincial level.

Article 78 The registered capital of a joint stock limited company shall be the total amount of paid-up share capital as registered with the Company Registration Authority.

The minimum registered capital of a joint stock limited company shall be RMB 10,000,000 yuan. If the minimum registered capital of a joint stock limited company needs to be higher than the aforesaid amount, it shall be stipulated separately by the laws, or administrative rules and regulations.

第七十九条 股份有限公司章程应当载明下列事项：

(一)公司名称和住所；

(二)公司经营范围；

(三)公司设立方式；

(四)公司股份总数、每股金额和注册资本；

(五)发起人的姓名或者名称、认购的股份数；

(六)股东的权利和义务；

(七)董事会的组成、职权、任期和议事规则；

(八)公司法定代表人；

(九)监事会的组成、职权、任期和议事规则；

(十)公司利润分配办法；

(十一)公司的解散事由与清算办法；

(十二)公司的通知和公告办法；

(十三)股东大会认为需要规定的其他事项。

第八十条 发起人可以用货币出资，也可以用实物、工业产权、非专利技术、土地使用权作价出资。对作为出资的实物、工业产权、非专利技术或者土地使用权，必须进行评估作价，核实财产，并折合为股份。不得高估或者低估作价。土地使用权的评估作价，依照法律、行政法规的规定办理。

Article 79 The articles of association of a joint stock limited company shall specify the following items:

(1) the name and domicile of the company;

(2) the scope of business of the company;

(3) the method of incorporation of the company;

(4) the total number of shares, the amount of each share and the registered capital of the company;

(5) the names or titles of the sponsors and the numbers of shares subscribed for by the sponsors;

(6) the rights and obligations of the shareholders;

(7) the composition, functions and powers, the term of office and the deliberation rules of the board of directors;

(8) the legal representative of the company;

(9) the composition, functions and powers, the term of office and the deliberation rules of the supervisory board;

(10) methods for the distribution of the company's profit;

(11) the reasons for dissolution of the company and liquidation method;

(12) methods for notices and announcements of the company; and

(13) other matters that the shareholders general meeting deems necessary to be specified.

Article 80 The sponsors may make their capital contributions in cash, or with material objects, industrial property rights, non-patented technology or land-use rights at their appraised value. Material objects, industrial property rights, non-patented technology or land-use rights contributed as capital must be appraised and valued, and such property must be verified and converted into shares. Such contributions may not be over-valued or under-valued. The appraisal and valuation of land-use rights shall be conducted in accordance with

发起人以工业产权、非专利技术作价出资的金额不得超过股份有限公司注册资本的百分之二十。

第八十一条　国有企业改建为股份有限公司时,严禁将国有资产低价折股、低价出售或者无偿分给个人。

第八十二条　以发起设立方式设立股份有限公司的,发起人以书面认足公司章程规定发行的股份后,应即缴纳全部股款;以实物、工业产权、非专利技术或者土地使用权抵作股款的,应当依法办理其财产权的转移手续。

发起人交付全部出资后,应当选举董事会和监事会,由董事会向公司登记机关报送设立公司的批准文件、公司章程、验资证明等文件,申请设立登记。

第八十三条　以募集设立方式设立股份有限公司的,发起人认购的股份不得少于公司股份总数的百分之三十五,其余股份应当向社会公开募集。

第八十四条　发起人向社会公开募集股份时,必须向国务院证券管理部门递交募股申请,并报送下列主要文件:

the provisions of the laws, administrative rules and regulations.

The amount of capital contributions made by sponsors in the form of industrial property rights and non-patented technology shall not exceed twenty percent of the registered capital of a joint stock limited company.

Article 81 Where a State-owned enterprise is restructured as a joint stock limited company, it shall be strictly prohibited to convert the State-owned assets into shares at a depressed price or to sell off them at a depressed price, or to distribute them to individuals without charge.

Article 82 Where a joint stock limited company is incorporated by means of sponsorship, the sponsors shall pay in full for their shares immediately after confirming in writing their subscription of the shares to be issued according to the articles of association of the company. If material objects, industrial property rights, non-patented technology or land-use rights are invested as payment for shares, the sponsors shall undertake the transfer procedures for property rights therein in accordance with the law.

After the sponsors make their capital contributions in full, they shall elect the board of directors and supervisory board. The board of directors shall submit to the Company Registration Authority the documents such as approval document for the company's incorporation, articles of association and capital verification certificate of the company, and shall apply for registration of incorporation.

Article 83 Where a joint stock limited company is incorporated by means of share offer, the sponsors shall not subscribe for less than thirty five percent of the total shares issued by the company, and the remaining shares shall be offered to the general public.

Article 84 When offering shares to the general public for subscription, the sponsors must submit to the department of security

(一)批准设立公司的文件；

(二)公司章程；

(三)经营估算书；

(四)发起人姓名或者名称,发起人认购的股份数、出资种类及验资证明；

(五)招股说明书；

(六)代收股款银行的名称及地址；

(七)承销机构名称及有关的协议。

未经国务院证券管理部门批准,发起人不得向社会公开募集股份。

第八十五条 经国务院证券管理部门批准,股份有限公司可以向境外公开募集股份,具体办法由国务院作出特别规定。

第八十六条 国务院证券管理部门对符合本法规定条件的募股申请,予以批准；对不符合本法规定的募股申请,不予批准。

对已作出的批准如发现不符合本法规定的,应予撤销。尚未募集股份的,停止募集；已经募集的,认股人可以按照所缴股款并加算银行同期存款利息,要求发起人返还。

administration under the State Council an application for share offer along with the following main documents:

(1) the approval documents for the incorporation of the company;

(2) the articles of association of the company;

(3) a business forecast;

(4) the names or titles of the sponsors, the number of shares subscribed for by the sponsors, the forms of capital contributions and the capital verification certificate;

(5) the prospectus on share offer;

(6) the name and address of the bank accepting subscription money on behalf of the company; and

(7) the name of the selling agencies and related agreements.

The sponsors shall not offer shares to the general public without the approval of the department of securities administration under the State Council.

Article 85 A joint stock limited company may, with the approval of the department of security administration under the State Council, offer its shares to the general public outside the territory of the People's Republic of China. The specific measures therefor shall be specially stipulated by the State Council.

Article 86 The department of security administration under the State Council shall approve the applications for share offer which conform to the stipulations of this Law, and disapprove the applications which fail to conform to the stipulations of this Law.

If an approval is found to be inconsistent with the stipulations of this Law after it has been granted, such approval shall be revoked. If the share offer has not yet been made, the offer shall be halted; if the share offer has already been made, the subscribers may claim a refund from the sponsors according to their paid-up subscriptions plus bank deposit interest calculated for the same period.

第八十七条　招股说明书应当附有发起人制订的公司章程,并载明下列事项:

(一)发起人认购的股份数;

(二)每股的票面金额和发行价格;

(三)无记名股票的发行总数;

(四)认股人的权利、义务;

(五)本次募股的起止期限及逾期未募足时认股人可撤回所认股份的说明。

第八十八条　发起人向社会公开募集股份,必须公告招股说明书,并制作认股书。认股书应当载明前条所列事项,由认股人填写所认股数、金额、住所,并签名、盖章。认股人按照所认股数缴纳股款。

第八十九条　发起人向社会公开募集股份,应当由依法设立的证券经营机构承销,签订承销协议。

第九十条　发起人向社会公开募集股份,应当同银行签订代收股款协议。

代收股款的银行应当按照协议代收和保存股款,向缴纳股款的认股人出具收款单据,并负有向有关部门出具收款证明的义务。

第九十一条　发行股份的股款缴足后,必须经法定的

Article 87 A prospectus on share offer shall have the articles of association of the company formulated by the sponsors attached, and shall specify the following:

(1) the number of shares subscribed for by the sponsors;

(2) the face value and the issue price of each share;

(3) the total number of bearer shares issued;

(4) the rights and obligations of the subscribers; and

(5) the term of the share offer and a statement to the effect that subscribers may withdraw their share subscriptions if all the shares are not taken up within the time limit.

Article 88 Where shares are to be offered to the general public, the sponsors must publish the company's prospectus on share offer and prepare subscription forms. The subscription forms shall contain the items listed in the preceding Article, and the subscribers shall fill in the number of shares subscribed for, the amount of money contributed to, and their respective domiciles on the forms, and shall sign and seal such forms. The subscribers shall pay their subscription money in accordance with the number of shares subscribed for.

Article 89 When sponsors offer shares to the public, the shares shall be distributed by a securities agency established according to law, with which a distribution agreement shall be concluded.

Article 90 Where shares are to be offered to the public, the sponsors shall enter into an agreement with a bank on the collection of subscription money on behalf of the company.

The bank entrusted with collecting the subscription money shall, in accordance with its agreement, collect and keep the subscription money, issue receipts to the subscribers for their payments, and bear an obligation to issue certification of receipt of subscription money to the relevant departments.

Article 91 After payment in full of the subscription money for

验资机构验资并出具证明。发起人应当在三十日内主持召开公司创立大会。创立大会由认股人组成。

发行的股份超过招股说明书规定的截止期限尚未募足的,或者发行股份的股款缴足后,发起人在三十日内未召开创立大会的,认股人可以按照所缴股款并加算银行同期存款利息,要求发起人返还。

第九十二条 发起人应当在创立大会召开十五日前将会议日期通知各认股人或者予以公告。创立大会应有代表股份总数二分之一以上的认股人出席,方可举行。

创立大会行使下列职权:

(一)审议发起人关于公司筹办情况的报告;

(二)通过公司章程;

(三)选举董事会成员;

(四)选举监事会成员;

(五)对公司的设立费用进行审核;

(六)对发起人用于抵作股款的财产的作价进行审核;

(七)发生不可抗力或者经营条件发生重大变化直接影

all shares is made, a statutory capital verification institution shall be commissioned to conduct a verification of the funds and produce a verification certificate. The sponsors shall, within thirty days thereafter, convene and preside over an inaugural meeting composed of all the subscribers.

If the number of shares has not been fully subscribed for within the time limit specified in the prospectus on share offer or, after payment in full of the subscription money for the total share is made, or if sponsors fail to hold an inaugural meeting within thirty days thereafter, the subscribers may claim a refund from the sponsors according to the paid-up share subscription money plus bank deposit interest calculated for the same period.

Article 92 The sponsors shall notify each subscriber of the date of the inaugural meeting or make a public announcement 15 days prior to the convening of the meeting. The inaugural meeting may be convened only if subscribers representing fifty percent or more of the total shares issued are present.

The following functions and powers shall be exercised at an inaugural meeting:

(1) to examine the sponsors report on the preparation for the incorporation of the company;

(2) to adopt the articles of association of the company;

(3) to elect members of the board of directors;

(4) to elect members of the supervisory board;

(5) to examine and verify the expenses incurred in the incorporation of the company;

(6) to examine and verify the valuation of the property used by the sponsors to pay for subscription money; and

(7) to resolve not to incorporate the company in the event that a force majeure or major changes in business operation conditions may

响公司设立的,可以作出不设立公司的决议。

创立大会对前款所列事项作出决议,必须经出席会议的认股人所持表决权的半数以上通过。

第九十三条 发起人、认股人缴纳股款或者交付抵作股款的出资后,除未按期募足股份、发起人未按期召开创立大会或者创立大会决议不设立公司的情形外,不得抽回其股本。

第九十四条 董事会应于创立大会结束后三十日内,向公司登记机关报送下列文件,申请设立登记:

(一)有关主管部门的批准文件;

(二)创立大会的会议记录;

(三)公司章程;

(四)筹办公司的财务审计报告;

(五)验资证明;

(六)董事会、监事会成员姓名及住所;

(七)法定代表人的姓名、住所。

第九十五条 公司登记机关自接到股份有限公司设立登记申请之日起三十日内作出是否予以登记的决定。对符合本法规定条件的,予以登记,发给公司营业执照;对不符

directly affect the incorporation of the company.

The resolution made at the inaugural meeting on the issues listed in the preceding paragraph must be approved by subscribers attending the meeting who represent more than half of the voting rights.

Article 93 Sponsors and subscribers may not withdraw their share capital after paying their subscription money or making their capital contributions as substitutes for subscription money, except where the total share issue is not fully subscribed for within the time limit or the sponsors fail to convene the inaugural meeting according to the schedule, or the inaugural meeting resolves not to incorporate the company.

Article 94 The board of directors shall, within thirty days after the inaugural meeting, submit the following documents to the Company Registration Authority and apply for registration of the incorporation of the company:

(1) the approval documents issued by the relevant department in charge;

(2) the minutes of the inaugural meeting;

(3) the articles of association of the company;

(4) the financial audit report on the preparation of the incorporation of the company;

(5) the capital verification certificate;

(6) the names and domiciles of the members of the board of directors and the supervisory board; and

(7) the name and domicile of the legal representative.

Article 95 The Company Registration Authority shall, within thirty days after receipt of an application for the incorporation of a joint stock limited company, make a decision whether or not to register the company. A company complying with the provisions of this Law shall be registered and a company business licence shall be issued thereto. A

合本法规定条件的,不予登记。

公司营业执照签发日期,为公司成立日期。公司成立后,应当进行公告。

股份有限公司经登记成立后,采取募集设立方式的,应当将募集股份情况报国务院证券管理部门备案。

第九十六条 设立股份有限公司的同时设立分公司的,应当就所设分公司向公司登记机关申请登记,领取营业执照。

股份有限公司成立后设立分公司,应当由公司法定代表人向公司登记机关申请登记,领取营业执照。

第九十七条 股份有限公司的发起人应当承担下列责任:

(一)公司不能成立时,对设立行为所产生的债务和费用负连带责任;

(二)公司不能成立时,对认股人已缴纳的股款,负返还股款并加算银行同期存款利息的连带责任;

(三)在公司设立过程中,由于发起人的过失致使公司利益受到损害的,应当对公司承担赔偿责任。

company failing to comply with the provisions of this Law shall not be registered.

The date of issuance of a company business licence shall be the date of the incorporation of the company. Once a company is incorporated, an announcement shall be made.

A joint stock limited company incorporated by means of share offer shall, after its registration for incorporation, report its share subscription to the department of security administration under the State Council for the record.

Article 96 Where branches are established simultaneously with the incorporation of a joint stock limited company, the company shall submit applications for registration of the establishment of the branches to, and obtain business licenses of the branches from, the Company Registration Authority.

Where branches are established after the incorporation of a joint stock limited company, the legal representative of the company shall submit applications for registration of the branches to, and obtain business licences of the branches from, the Company Registration Authority.

Article 97 The sponsors of a joint stock limited company shall bear the following responsibilities:

(1) in the event of the company failing to be incorporated, joint and several liabilities for all debts and expenses incurred in the act of the incorporation;

(2) in the event of the company failing to be incorporated, joint and several liabilities for refunding to the subscribers the paid-up subscription money plus bank deposit interest calculated for the same period of time; and

(3) in the event of the interests of the company being damaged during the course of its incorporation due to fault of the sponsors, liability for compensation to the company.

第九十八条　有限责任公司变更为股份有限公司,应当符合本法规定的股份有限公司的条件,并依照本法有关设立股份有限公司的程序办理。

第九十九条　有限责任公司依法经批准变更为股份有限公司时,折合的股份总额应当相等于公司净资产额。有限责任公司依法经批准变更为股份有限公司,为增加资本向社会公开募集股份时,应当依照本法有关向社会公开募集股份的规定办理。

第一百条　有限责任公司依法变更为股份有限公司的,原有限责任公司的债权、债务由变更后的股份有限公司承继。

第一百零一条　股份有限公司应当将公司章程、股东名册、股东大会会议记录、财务会计报告置备于本公司。

第二节　股东大会

第一百零二条　股份有限公司由股东组成股东大会。股东大会是公司的权力机构,依照本法行使职权。

第一百零三条　股东大会行使下列职权:

Article 98 If a limited liability company is to be converted into a joint stock limited company, it shall satisfy the requirements for a joint stock limited company stipulated by this Law and the conversion shall be handled in accordance with the procedures stipulated in this Law for the incorporation of a joint stock limited company.

Article 99 Where a limited liability company is, after approval, converted into a joint stock limited company in accordance with the law, the total amount of its shares converted shall be equal to the amount of its net assets. Where a limited liability company that is, after approval, converted into a joint stock limited company in accordance with the law offers shares to the general public for the purpose of increasing its capital, it shall be handled in accordance with the provisions of this Law in respect of the share offers to the public.

Article 100 Where a limited liability company is converted into a joint stock limited company in accordance with the law, the claims and debts of the original limited liability company shall be succeeded to by the joint stock limited company into which it is converted.

Article 101 A joint stock limited company shall keep its articles of association, roster of the shareholders, minutes of the shareholders general meetings and financial and accounting statements at the company.

Section 2 Shareholders' General Meetings

Article 102 A joint stock limited company shall form a shareholders general meeting which shall be composed of all the shareholders. The shareholders general meeting is the organ of power of the company and shall exercise its functions and powers in accordance with this Law.

Article 103 The shareholders' general meeting shall exercise the

（一）决定公司的经营方针和投资计划；

（二）选举和更换董事，决定有关董事的报酬事项；

（三）选举和更换由股东代表出任的监事，决定有关监事的报酬事项；

（四）审议批准董事会的报告；

（五）审议批准监事会的报告；

（六）审议批准公司的年度财务预算方案、决算方案；

（七）审议批准公司的利润分配方案和弥补亏损方案；

（八）对公司增加或者减少注册资本作出决议；

（九）对发行公司债券作出决议；

（十）对公司合并、分立、解散和清算等事项作出决议；

（十一）修改公司章程。

第一百零四条 股东大会应当每年召开一次年会。有下列情形之一的，应当在二个月内召开临时股东大会：

（一）董事人数不足本法规定的人数或者公司章程所定人数的三分之二时；

（二）公司未弥补的亏损达股本总额三分之一时；

（三）持有公司股份百分之十以上的股东请求时；

following functions and powers:

(1) to decide upon policies on business operation and investment plans of the company;

(2) to elect and replace members of the board of directors and to decide upon matters concerning the remuneration of the directors;

(3) to elect and replace the supervisors who are representatives of the shareholders and to decide upon matters concerning the remuneration of the supervisors;

(4) to examine and approve reports of the board of directors;

(5) to examine and approve reports of the supervisory board;

(6) to examine and approve plans of the company's fiscal financial budget and final accounts;

(7) to examine and approve plans for company's profit distribution and making up losses;

(8) to make resolutions on the increase or reduction of the registered capital of the company;

(9) to adopt resolutions on the issuance of company bonds;

(10) to adopt resolutions on matters such as the merger, division, dissolution and liquidation of the company; and

(11) to amend the articles of association of the company.

Article 104 The annual meeting of the shareholders general meeting shall be convened once a year. An interim shareholders general meeting shall be convened within two months if any of the following situations occurs:

(1) if the number of directors is less than the number stipulated by this Law, or less than two-thirds of the number required by the articles of association of the company;

(2) if the amount of the company's losses that have not been made up reaches one-third of its total share capital;

(3) if shareholders holding ten percent or more of the company's

(四)董事会认为必要时;

(五)监事会提议召开时。

第一百零五条 股东大会会议由董事会依照本法规定负责召集,由董事长主持。董事长因特殊原因不能履行职务时,由董事长指定的副董事长或者其他董事主持。召开股东大会,应当将会议审议的事项于会议召开三十日以前通知各股东。临时股东大会不得对通知中未列明的事项作出决议。

发行无记名股票的,应当于会议召开四十五日以前就前款事项作出公告。

无记名股票持有人出席股东大会的,应当于会议召开五日以前至股东大会闭会时止将股票交存于公司。

第一百零六条 股东出席股东大会,所持每一股份有一表决权。

股东大会作出决议,必须经出席会议的股东所持表决权的半数以上通过。股东大会对公司合并、分立或者解散公司作出决议,必须经出席会议的股东所持表决权的三分之二以上通过。

第一百零七条 修改公司章程必须经出席股东大会的

shares request to convene a shareholders meeting;

(4) if the board of directors deems it necessary; and

(5) if the supervisory board proposes that such a meeting be convened.

Article 105 A shareholders general meeting shall be convened by the board of directors in accordance with the provisions of this Law and presided over by the Chairman of the board. Where the Chairman is unable to perform his duties due to special reasons, the vice-chairman or other director designated by the Chairman may preside over such meetings. Shareholders shall be notified of the matters to be considered at a shareholders general meeting thirty days prior to the holding of such a meeting. At interim shareholders general meetings, no resolutions may be adopted in respect of matters not included in the notice.

Where bearer shares are to be issued, a public announcement shall be made in respect of the matters mentioned in the preceding paragraph forty-five days prior to the holding of such a meeting.

Holders of bearer shares attending the shareholders general meeting shall deposit their share certificates with the company for the period from five days prior to the holding of the meeting until the end of the meeting.

Article 106 Shareholders attending a shareholders general meeting shall have the right to one vote for each share held.

A resolution of the shareholders general meeting must be . passed by more than one half of the voting rights held by the shareholders present at the meeting. Resolutions on the merger, division or dissolution of the company adopted by the shareholders general meeting must require more than two-thirds of the voting rights held by the shareholders present at the meeting.

Article 107 Amendments to the articles of association of the

股东所持表决权的三分之二以上通过。

第一百零八条　股东可以委托代理人出席股东大会,代理人应当向公司提交股东授权委托书,并在授权范围内行使表决权。

第一百零九条　股东大会应当对所议事项的决定作成会议记录,由出席会议的董事签名。会议记录应当与出席股东的签名册及代理出席的委托书一并保存。

第一百一十条　股东有权查阅公司章程、股东大会会议记录和财务会计报告,对公司的经营提出建议或者质询。

第一百一十一条　股东大会、董事会的决议违反法律、行政法规,侵犯股东合法权益的,股东有权向人民法院提起要求停止该违法行为和侵害行为的诉讼。

第三节　董事会、经理

第一百一十二条　股份有限公司设董事会,其成员为五人至十九人。

董事会对股东大会负责,行使下列职权:

(一)负责召集股东大会,并向股东大会报告工作;

company must be adopted by more than two-thirds of the voting rights held by the shareholders present at the shareholders general meeting.

Article 108 A shareholder may entrust a proxy to attend the shareholders general meeting on his behalf. The proxy shall present the shareholders power of attorney to the company and exercise voting rights within the scope of authorization.

Article 109 Resolutions on matters discussed at a shareholders general meeting shall be minuted down. The directors attending the meeting shall sign the minutes. The minutes of the meeting shall be kept together with the roster of the signatures of the shareholders attending the meeting and the powers of attorney of attending proxies.

Article 110 Shareholders shall have the right to examine the articles of association of the company, the minutes of the shareholders general meetings and the financial and accounting statements, and to make suggestions or inquiries about the business operation of the company.

Article 111 Where a resolution of the shareholders general meeting or of the board of directors violates the law or administrative rules and regulations or infringes the lawful rights and interests of the shareholders, the shareholders concerned shall have the right to bring a lawsuit in a people's court demanding that such illegal or infringing action be stopped.

Section 3 Board of Directors and Manager

Article 112 A joint stock limited company shall have a board of directors composed of five to nineteen members.

The board of directors shall be responsible to the shareholders general meeting and exercise the following functions and powers:

(1) to convene the shareholders' general meeting and to report on

(二)执行股东大会的决议;

(三)决定公司的经营计划和投资方案;

(四)制订公司的年度财务预算方案、决算方案;

(五)制订公司的利润分配方案和弥补亏损方案;

(六)制订公司增加或者减少注册资本的方案以及发行公司债券的方案;

(七)拟订公司合并、分立、解散的方案;

(八)决定公司内部管理机构的设置;

(九)聘任或者解聘公司经理,根据经理的提名,聘任或者解聘公司副经理、财务负责人,决定其报酬事项;

(十)制定公司的基本管理制度。

第一百一十三条 董事会设董事长一人,可以设副董事长一至二人。董事长和副董事长由董事会以全体董事的过半数选举产生。

董事长为公司的法定代表人。

第一百一十四条 董事长行使下列职权:

(一)主持股东大会和召集、主持董事会会议;

its work to the shareholders general meeting;

(2) to implement resolutions passed at the shareholders general meetings;

(3) to decide on the business operation plans and the investment plans of the company;

(4) to formulate the fiscal financial budgets and the final accounts of the company;

(5) to formulate plans for the profit distribution and making up losses of the company;

(6) to formulate plans for increasing or reducing the registered capital of the company and plans for the issue of company bonds;

(7) to formulate plans for the merger, division and dissolution of the company;

(8) to decide on the establishment of the internal management organs of the company;

(9) to engage or dismiss the manager and, upon recommendation of the manager, to engage or dismiss the deputy manager (s) and responsible persons in charge of the financial affairs of the company, and to decide on matters concerning their remuneration; and

(10) to formulate the basic managment system of the company.

Article 113 The board of directors shall have one chairman and may have one or two vice-chairmen. The chairman and vice-chairmen of the board of directors shall be elected by the affirmative votes of more than half of all the directors.

The chairman of the board shall be the legal representative of the company.

Article 114 The chairman of the board shall exercise the following functions and powers:

(1) to preside over shareholders general meetings, and to convene and preside over meetings of the board of directors;

(二)检查董事会决议的实施情况；

(三)签署公司股票、公司债券。

副董事长协助董事长工作,董事长不能履行职权时,由董事长指定的副董事长代行其职权。

第一百一十五条 董事任期由公司章程规定,但每届任期不得超过三年。董事任期届满,连选可以连任。

董事在任期届满前,股东大会不得无故解除其职务。

第一百一十六条 董事会每年度至少召开二次会议,每次会议应当于会议召开十日以前通知全体董事。

董事会召开临时会议,可以另定召集董事会的通知方式和通知时限。

第一百一十七条 董事会会议应由二分之一以上的董事出席方可举行。董事会作出决议,必须经全体董事的过半数通过。

第一百一十八条 董事会会议,应由董事本人出席。董事因故不能出席,可以书面委托其他董事代为出席董事会,委托书中应载明授权范围。

董事会应当对会议所议事项的决定作成会议记录,出

(2) to examine the implementation of resolutions of the board of directors; and

(3) to sign the shares and the bonds of the company.

The vice-chairmen of the board shall assist the chairman of the board in his work and shall, upon designation by the chairman, exercise the chairman's powers and functions on behalf of the chairman of the board in case the chairman is unable to perform his powers and functions.

Article 115 The term of office of the directors shall be stipulated in the articles of association of the company, but each term shall not exceed three years. A director may serve consecutive terms if reelected upon expiration of his term of office.

The shareholders general meeting may not without reason remove a director from office before the expiration of his term of office.

Article 116 Meetings of the board of directors shall be held at least twice a year. All the members of the board shall be notified of the meeting ten days prior to the holding of the meeting.

The notification method and time limit for giving notice of the convening of the interim meetings of the board of directors may be separately decided.

Article 117 A meeting of the board of directors shall be convened only if more than one half of all the directors are present. Any resolution of the board must be adopted by the affirmative votes of more than one half of all the directors.

Article 118 Meetings of the board of directors shall be attended by the directors in person. If a director is unable to attend a meeting of the board for certain reasons, he may entrust another director in writing with attending the meeting on his behalf. The power of attorney shall define the scope of authorization.

Decisions on matters discussed at a meeting of the board of

席会议的董事和记录员在会议记录上签名。

董事应当对董事会的决议承担责任。董事会的决议违反法律、行政法规或者公司章程,致使公司遭受严重损失的,参与决议的董事对公司负赔偿责任。但经证明在表决时曾表明异议并记载于会议记录的,该董事可以免除责任。

第一百一十九条 股份有限公司设经理,由董事会聘任或者解聘。经理对董事会负责,行使下列职权:

(一)主持公司的生产经营管理工作,组织实施董事会决议;

(二)组织实施公司年度经营计划和投资方案;

(三)拟订公司内部管理机构设置方案;

(四)拟订公司的基本管理制度;

(五)制定公司的具体规章;

(六)提请聘任或者解聘公司副经理、财务负责人;

(七)聘任或者解聘除应由董事会聘任或者解聘以外的负责管理人员;

(八)公司章程和董事会授予的其他职权。

directors shall be minuted. Such minutes of the meeting shall be signed by the directors and clerks present.

Directors shall be responsible for resolutions passed by the board of directors. If a resolution of the board violates the law, administrative rules and regulations or the articles of association of the company and thus causes serious losses to the company, the directors who participated in the adoption of such a resolution shall be liable for compensation to the company. However, if a director is proved to have expressed his objection to such a resolution when it was put to the vote and his objection was recorded in the minutes of the meeting, he may be exempted from such liability.

Article 119 A joint stock limited company shall have a manager, who shall be engaged or dismissed by the board of directors. The manager shall be responsible to the board of directors and shall exercise the following functions and powers:

(1) to be in charge of the production, operation and management of the company and to organize the implementation of resolutions of the board of directors;

(2) to organize the implementation of the annual business plans and investment plans of the company;

(3) to draft plans for the establishment of internal management organs of the company;

(4) to draft the basic management system of the company;

(5) to formulate specific rules and regulations of the company;

(6) to propose the appointment or dismissal of deputy manager(s) and responsible persons in charge of the financial affairs of the company;

(7) to appoint or dismiss management personnel, except those who shall be appointed or dismissed by the board of directors; and

(8) to exercise other functions and powers authorized by the

经理列席董事会会议。

第一百二十条 公司根据需要,可以由董事会授权董事长在董事会闭会期间,行使董事会的部分职权。

公司董事会可以决定,由董事会成员兼任经理。

第一百二十一条 公司研究决定有关职工工资、福利、安全生产以及劳动保护、劳动保险等涉及职工切身利益的问题,应当事先听取公司工会和职工的意见,并邀请工会或者职工代表列席有关会议。

第一百二十二条 公司研究决定生产经营的重大问题、制定重要的规章制度时,应当听取公司工会和职工的意见和建议。

第一百二十三条 董事、经理应当遵守公司章程,忠实履行职务,维护公司利益,不得利用在公司的地位和职权为自己谋取私利。

本法第五十七条至第六十三条有关不得担任董事、经理的规定以及董事、经理义务、责任的规定,适用于股份有限公司的董事、经理。

articles of association of the company and by the board of directors.

The manager shall attend meetings of the board of directors as a non-voting participant.

Article 120　If necessary, the board of directors may authorize its chairman to perform part of its functions and powers when the meeting of the board is not in session.

The board of directors may decide that one of its members shall concurrently serve as the manager of the company.

Article 121　A company shall solicit in advance the opinions of the trade union and its staff and workers in studying and deciding on issues involving the personal interests of its staff and workers such as the salary, welfare, safety in production, labour protection and labour insurance, and shall invite representatives from the trade union or from its staff and workers to attend relevant meetings as non-voting participants.

Article 122　A company shall solicit the opinions and suggestions of the trade union and its staff and workers when studying and deciding major issues in respect of the company's production and operations or the formulation of important rules and regulations of the company.

Article 123　Directors and managers shall abide by the articles of association of the company, faithfully perform their duties and protect the interests of the company, and shall not use their positions, functions and powers in the company to seek personal gains.

Provisions of Articles 57 to 63 of this Law regarding persons disqualified to serve as directors and managers, and the obligations and responsibilities of the directors and managers shall apply to directors and managers of joint stock limited companies.

第四节 监 事 会

第一百二十四条 股份有限公司设监事会,其成员不得少于三人。监事会应在其组成人员中推选一名召集人。

监事会由股东代表和适当比例的公司职工代表组成,具体比例由公司章程规定。监事会中的职工代表由公司职工民主选举产生。

董事、经理及财务负责人不得兼任监事。

第一百二十五条 监事的任期每届为三年。监事任期届满,连选可以连任。

第一百二十六条 监事会行使下列职权:

(一)检查公司的财务;

(二)对董事、经理执行公司职务时违反法律、法规或者公司章程的行为进行监督;

(三)当董事和经理的行为损害公司的利益时,要求董事和经理予以纠正;

(四)提议召开临时股东大会;

(五)公司章程规定的其他职权。

Section 4 Supervisory Board

Article 124 A joint stock limited company shall have a supervisory board composed of no less than three members. The supervisory board shall elect a convener from among its members.

The supervisory board shall be composed of shareholders' representatives and an appropriate proportion of representatives of the staff and workers of the company, and the specific proportion of such representatives shall be provided for by the articles of association of the company. The representatives of the staff and workers serving on the supervisory board shall be democratically elected by the staff and workers of the company.

Directors, managers and responsible persons in charge of the financial affairs of the company may not serve concurrently as supervisors.

Article 125 The term of office of the supervisors shall be three years. A supervisor may serve consecutive terms if re-elected upon expiration of his term of office.

Article 126 A supervisory board shall exercise the following functions and powers:

(1) to examine the financial affairs of the company;

(2) to supervise the acts of the directors and the manager violating the laws, the administrative rules and regulations or the articles of association of the company during the performance of their functions;

(3) to demand directors or the manager to make corrections if any of their acts is found to have damaged the interests of the company;

(4) to propose the convening of interim shareholders general meetings; and

(5) other functions and powers provided for in the articles of

监事列席董事会会议。

第一百二十七条 监事会的议事方式和表决程序由公司章程规定。

第一百二十八条 监事应当依照法律、行政法规、公司章程,忠实履行监督职责。

本法第五十七条至第五十九条、第六十二条至第六十三条有关不得担任监事的规定以及监事义务、责任的规定,适用于股份有限公司的监事。

第四章 股份有限公司的股份发行和转让

第一节 股份发行

第一百二十九条 股份有限公司的资本划分为股份,每一股的金额相等。

公司的股份采取股票的形式。股票是公司签发的证明股东所持股份的凭证。

第一百三十条 股份的发行,实行公开、公平、公正的原则,必须同股同权,同股同利。

同次发行的股票,每股的发行条件和价格应当相同。

association of the company.

Supervisors shall attend meetings of the board of directors as non-voting participants.

Article 127 The articles of association of the company shall stipulate the method of deliberation and voting procedures of the supervisory board.

Article 128 A supervisor shall faithfully perform his duties of supervision in accordance with the law, the administrative rules and regulations and the articles of association of the company.

Provisions of Articles 57 to 59 and Articles 62 to 63 of this Law regarding persons disqualified to serve as supervisors and the obligations and responsibilities of supervisors shall apply to the supervisors of joint stock limited companies.

Chapter IV Issue and Transfer of Shares of Joint Stock Limited Companies

Section 1 Issue of Shares

Article 129 The capital of a joint stock limited company shall be divided into shares of equal value.

The shares of the company shall take the form of share certificates, which are vouchers issued by the company to certify the shares held by their shareholders.

Article 130 The issue of shares shall be in compliance with the principles of publicity, fairness and justice. The same shares must carry the same rights and the same benefits.

Shares of the same issue shall be issued on the same conditions and

任何单位或者个人所认购的股份,每股应当支付相同价额。

第一百三十一条 股票发行价格可以按票面金额,也可以超过票面金额,但不得低于票面金额。

以超过票面金额为股票发行价格的,须经国务院证券管理部门批准。

以超过票面金额发行股票所得溢价款列入公司资本公积金。

股票溢价发行的具体管理办法由国务院另行规定。

第一百三十二条 股票采用纸面形式或者国务院证券管理部门规定的其他形式。

股票应当载明下列主要事项:

(一)公司名称;

(二)公司登记成立的日期;

(三)股票种类、票面金额及代表的股份数;

(四)股票的编号。

股票由董事长签名,公司盖章。

发起人的股票,应当标明发起人股票字样。

第一百三十三条 公司向发起人、国家授权投资的机构、法人发行的股票,应当为记名股票,并应当记载该发起人、机构或者法人的名称,不得另立户名或者以代表人姓名记名。

at the same price. A unit or an individual subscribing to shares shall pay the same price for each share.

Article 131 Shares may be issued at or above par but not below par.

Shares to be issued above par shall be subjected to the approval of the department of security administration under the State Council.

The premiums generated from issuing shares above par shall be entered under the capital common reserve fund of the company.

Specific measures for the administration of issue of shares above par shall be separately stipulated by the State Council.

Article 132 Share certificates may be in paper form or in such other forms as stipulated by the department of security administration under the State Council.

The following main particulars shall be clearly stated on a share certificate:

(1) the name of the company;

(2) the date of registration of the company's incorporation;

(3) the class of the shares, the par value and the number of shares represented by the certificate; and

(4) the serial number of the share certificate.

A share certificate shall be signed by the chairman of the board of directors and sealed with the seal of the company.

In the case of share certificates owned by sponsors, the words "sponsor's share certificate" shall be clearly stated on the share certificates.

Article 133 Shares issued by a company to sponsors, a State-authorized investment institution or legal persons shall be registered shares which shall state the names of the sponsors, State-authorized investment institution or legal persons. Such shares may not be registered in other names, or names of their representatives.

对社会公众发行的股票,可以为记名股票,也可以为无记名股票。

第一百三十四条 公司发行记名股票的,应当置备股东名册,记载下列事项:

(一)股东的姓名或者名称及住所;

(二)各股东所持股份数;

(三)各股东所持股票的编号;

(四)各股东取得其股份的日期。

发行无记名股票的,公司应当记载其股票数量、编号及发行日期。

第一百三十五条 国务院可以对公司发行本法规定的股票以外的其他种类的股票,另行作出规定。

第一百三十六条 股份有限公司登记成立后,即向股东正式交付股票。公司登记成立前不得向股东交付股票。

第一百三十七条 公司发行新股,必须具备下列条件:

(一)前一次发行的股份已募足,并间隔一年以上;

(二)公司在最近三年内连续盈利,并可向股东支付股利;

(三)公司在最近三年内财务会计文件无虚假记载;

(四)公司预期利润率可达同期银行存款利率。

Shares issued to the general public may be either registered shares or bearer shares.

Article 134 Where registered shares are issued, the company shall prepare a roster of the shareholders, in which the following items shall be recorded:

(1) the names or titles, and domiciles of the shareholders;

(2) the number of shares held by each shareholder;

(3) the serial numbers of the share certificates held by each shareholder; and

(4) the date on which each shareholder obtained his shares.

Where bearer shares are issued, the company shall keep a record of the number, the serial numbers and the issue date of the share certificates.

Article 135 The State Council may formulate separate regulations on the issue of other classes of shares which are not provided for in this Law.

Article 136 A joint stock limited company shall formally deliver share certificates to its shareholders immediately after the registration of its incorporation. No company may deliver share certificates to its shareholders prior to the registration of its incorporation.

Article 137 To issue new shares, a company must satisfy the following conditions:

(1) shares of the previous issue must have fully been subscribed for and at least one year has elapsed since the previous issue of shares;

(2) the company has been continuously profitable for the last three years and is able to pay dividends to its shareholders;

(3) the company is not found to have false records in the financial accounting documents in the last three years; and

(4) the forecast profit rate of the company can reach the interest rate of bank deposit for the same period of time.

公司以当年利润分派新股,不受前款第(二)项限制。

第一百三十八条 公司发行新股,股东大会应当对下列事项作出决议:

(一)新股种类及数额;

(二)新股发行价格;

(三)新股发行的起止日期;

(四)向原有股东发行新股的种类及数额。

第一百三十九条 股东大会作出发行新股的决议后,董事会必须向国务院授权的部门或者省级人民政府申请批准。属于向社会公开募集的,须经国务院证券管理部门批准。

第一百四十条 公司经批准向社会公开发行新股时,必须公告新股招股说明书和财务会计报表及附属明细表,并制作认股书。

公司向社会公开发行新股,应当由依法设立的证券经营机构承销,签订承销协议。

第一百四十一条 公司发行新股,可根据公司连续盈利情况和财产增值情况,确定其作价方案。

第一百四十二条 公司发行新股募足股款后,必须向

A company's distribution of new shares from the current year's profits shall not be restricted by item (2) of the preceding paragraph.

Article 138 Where a company issues new shares, resolutions on the following matters shall be adopted by a shareholders general meeting:

(1) the class and number of the new shares;

(2) the issue price of the new shares;

(3) the opening and closing dates of the new share issue; and

(4) the class and number of new shares issued to existing shareholders.

Article 139 After the shareholders general meeting adopts a resolution to issue new shares, the board of directors must apply to the department authorized by the State Council or to the local provincial people's government for approval. If the new shares are to be issued to the general public, the approval of the department of security administration under the State Council must be obtained.

Article 140 When a company obtains the approval to issue new shares to the general public, it must publicly announce its prospectus on new share offer and its financial accounting statements with annexed detailed schedules, and shall prepare subscription application forms.

When a company issues new shares openly to the public, the new shares shall be distributed by a securities agency established in accordance with the law, with which a distribution agreement shall be concluded.

Article 141 Where a company issues new shares, it may determine the pricing proposal for new shares based upon the circumstances of its consecutive profit gains and property value appreciations.

Article 142 Where the new share issue of a company is fully

公司登记机关办理变更登记,并公告。

第二节 股份转让

第一百四十三条 股东持有的股份可以依法转让。

第一百四十四条 股东转让其股份,必须在依法设立的证券交易场所进行。

第一百四十五条 记名股票,由股东以背书方式或者法律、行政法规规定的其他方式转让。

记名股票的转让,由公司将受让人的姓名或者名称及住所记载于股东名册。

股东大会召开前三十日内或者公司决定分配股利的基准日前五日内,不得进行前款规定的股东名册的变更登记。

第一百四十六条 无记名股票的转让,由股东在依法设立的证券交易场所将该股票交付给受让人后即发生转让的效力。

第一百四十七条 发起人持有的本公司股份,自公司成立之日起三年内不得转让。

公司董事、监事、经理应当向公司申报所持有的本公司的股份,并在任职期间内不得转让。

subscribed for, the company shall apply to the Company Registration Authority for registration of the modification in its capital and make a public announcement thereafter.

Section 2 Transfer of Shares

Article 143 Shares held by shareholders may be transferred in accordance with the law.

Article 144 Transfer of shares by shareholders shall be conducted through stock exchanges established in accordance with the law.

Article 145 Registered shares shall be transferred by means of endorsement by the shareholders or by such other means as provided for by the law and administrative rules and regulations.

When registered shares are transferred, the company shall register the transferee's name or title and domicile in its roster of shareholders.

No registration of modification to the roster of shareholders as stipulated in the preceding paragraph shall be made within thirty days prior to the convening of a shareholders general meeting or within five days prior to the date decided by the company for the distribution of dividends.

Article 146 Transfer of bearer shares shall become effective immediately after the shareholder delivers the share certificates to the transferee at a stock exchange established in accordance with the law.

Article 147 Shares held by the sponsors of a company shall not be transferred within three years after the date of incorporation of the company.

Directors, supervisors and the manager shall declare their numbers of shares held by them to the company, and shall not transfer such shares during their term of office.

第一百四十八条 国家授权投资的机构可以依法转让其持有的股份,也可以购买其他股东持有的股份。转让或者购买股份的审批权限、管理办法,由法律、行政法规另行规定。

第一百四十九条 公司不得收购本公司的股票,但为减少公司资本而注销股份或者与持有本公司股票的其他公司合并时除外。

公司依照前款规定收购本公司的股票后,必须在十日内注销该部分股份,依照法律、行政法规办理变更登记,并公告。

公司不得接受本公司的股票作为抵押权的标的。

第一百五十条 记名股票被盗、遗失或者灭失,股东可以依照民事诉讼法规定的公示催告程序,请求人民法院宣告该股票失效。

依照公示催告程序,人民法院宣告该股票失效后,股东可以向公司申请补发股票。

第三节 上市公司

第一百五十一条 本法所称上市公司是指所发行的股

Article 148 The State-authorized investment institution may transfer its shares held by it in accordance with the law and may purchase shares held by other shareholders. The authority to examine and approve such transfers or purchases and measures for administration thereof shall be separately provided for by the law and administrative rules and regulations.

Article 149 A company may not purchase its own shares except where, for the purpose of reducing its capital, shares need to be cancelled, or where the company merges with another company which holds its shares.

A company must cancel the shares purchased by the company itself in accordance with the preceding paragraph within ten days, and register the change of its capital in accordance with laws and administrative rules and regulations and make a public announcement thereafter.

A company may not accept its own shares as the subject matter of a mortgage.

Article 150 Where registered share certificates are stolen, lost or destroyed, the shareholder may, in accordance with the procedure for publicizing public notice for assertion of claims provided for in the Civil Procedure Law, request a people's court to declare such share certificates as void.

After the voidance has been declared by a people's court in accordance with the aforesaid procedure, the shareholder may apply to the company for a replacement of the share certificates.

Section 3 Listed Companies

Article 151 A listed company mentioned in this Law refers to a joint stock limited company which has its issued shares listed and

票经国务院或者国务院授权证券管理部门批准在证券交易所上市交易的股份有限公司。

第一百五十二条 股份有限公司申请其股票上市必须符合下列条件：

（一）股票经国务院证券管理部门批准已向社会公开发行；

（二）公司股本总额不少于人民币五千万元；

（三）开业时间在三年以上，最近三年连续盈利；原国有企业依法改建而设立的，或者本法实施后新组建成立，其主要发起人为国有大中型企业的，可连续计算；

（四）持有股票面值达人民币一千元以上的股东人数不少于一千人，向社会公开发行的股份达公司股份总数的百分之二十五以上；公司股本总额超过人民币四亿元的，其向社会公开发行股份的比例为百分之十五以上；

（五）公司在最近三年内无重大违法行为，财务会计报告无虚假记载；

（六）国务院规定的其他条件。

第一百五十三条 股份有限公司申请其股票上市交

traded at stock exchanges with the approval of the State Council or the department of securities administration authorized by the State Council.

Article 152 Where a joint stock limited company applies to have its shares listed and traded, the following conditions shall be satisfied:

(1) the shares have already been issued to the general public with approval of the securities administration department under the State Council;

(2) the total amount of the company's share capital reaches not less than RMB 50,000,000 yuan;

(3) the Company must have been in operation for three years or more and have made profits for the past three consecutive years; the business operation of a company which is converted from a State-owned enterprise according to law or which is newly incorporated after the implementation of this Law with medium and large-sized State-owned enterprises as the main sponsors may be traced back without interruption to the original enterprise or the main sponsors;

(4) the number of shareholders holding shares at the face value of RMB1,000 yuan or more is not less than one thousand and the shares issued to the general public amount to twenty five percent or more of the total share issue; where the company has a registered capital of more than RMB400,000,000 yuan, the ratio of shares issued to the general public must amount to fifteen percent or more of the total share issue;

(5) the company must have no records of involvement in serious illegal activities in the recent three years, and its financial accounting statements must contain no false information in the same period; and

(6) other conditions as stipulated by the State Council.

Article 153 Where a joint stock limited company applies to have its shares listed and traded in a stock exchange, it shall apply to the

易,应当报经国务院或者国务院授权证券管理部门批准,依照有关法律、行政法规的规定报送有关文件。

国务院或者国务院授权证券管理部门对符合本法规定条件的股票上市交易申请,予以批准;对不符合本法规定条件的,不予批准。

股票上市交易申请经批准后,被批准的上市公司必须公告其股票上市报告,并将其申请文件存放在指定的地点供公众查阅。

第一百五十四条 经批准的上市公司的股份,依照有关法律、行政法规上市交易。

第一百五十五条 经国务院证券管理部门批准,公司股票可以到境外上市,具体办法由国务院作出特别规定。

第一百五十六条 上市公司必须按照法律、行政法规的规定,定期公开其财务状况和经营情况,在每会计年度内半年公布一次财务会计报告。

第一百五十七条 上市公司有下列情形之一的,由国务院证券管理部门决定暂停其股票上市:

(一)公司股本总额、股权分布等发生变化不再具备上市条件;

State Council or the department of security administration authorized by the State Council for approval and submit the relevant documents as required by the law and administrative rules and regulations.

The State Council or the department of security administration authorized by the State Council shall approve applications for approval of the listing and trading of shares that comply with the conditions specified in this Law and shall not approve those that fail to comply with the provisions of this Law.

Where an application for the listing and trading of shares has been approved, the approved listed company must publicly announce its report on the listing of its shares and put its application documents at a designated place for public review.

Article 154 Shares of an approved listed company shall be listed and traded in accordance with the relevant laws and administrative rules and regulations.

Article 155 Upon approval of the department of security administration under the State Council, shares of a joint stock limited company may be listed and traded in stock exchanges outside the territory of the People's Republic of China and the measures therefor shall be specially formulated by the State Council.

Article 156 A listed company must, in compliance with the provisions of the laws and administrative rules and regulations, regularly disclose its financial and business situations. A financial accounting report shall be publicized every half year of each fiscal year.

Article 157 The department of security administration under the State Council may decide to suspend the listing of the shares of a listed company if any of the following circumstances occurs:

(1) the total share capital and the distribution of share ownership have been altered to make the company no longer satisfy the requirements necessary for listing;

（二）公司不按规定公开其财务状况,或者对财务会计报告作虚假记载;

（三）公司有重大违法行为;

（四）公司最近三年连续亏损。

第一百五十八条 上市公司有前条第(二)项、第(三)项所列情形之一经查实后果严重的,或者有前条第(一)项、第(四)项所列情形之一,在限期内未能消除,不具备上市条件的,由国务院证券管理部门决定终止其股票上市。

公司决议解散、被行政主管部门依法责令关闭或者被宣告破产的,由国务院证券管理部门决定终止其股票上市。

第五章　公司债券

第一百五十九条 股份有限公司、国有独资公司和两个以上的国有企业或者其他两个以上的国有投资主体投资设立的有限责任公司,为筹集生产经营资金,可以依照本法发行公司债券。

第一百六十条 本法所称公司债券是指公司依照法定

(2) the company has failed to make public its financial situation in compliance with the legal provisions or has falsified its financial accounting statements;

(3) the company is involved in major illegal acts; or

(4) the company has incurred losses for the past three consecutive years.

Article 158 Where any of the circumstances stipulated in item (2) or (3) of the preceding Article applies to a listed company and the consequences are verified to be serious, or where any of the circumstances stipulated in item (1) or (4) of the preceding Article is unable to be eliminated within the time limit and the company has become disqualified as a listed company, the department of security administration under the State Council shall decide to terminate the listing of the shares of the company.

Where a company decides to dissolve itself, is ordered by a competent administrative department in accordance with the law to close down or is declared bankrupt, the department of security administration under the State Council shall decide to terminate the listing of the company's shares.

Chapter V Company Bonds

Article 159 A joint stock limited company, a wholly State-owned company, and a limited liability company incorporated by two or more State-owned enterprises or by two or more other State-owned investment entities may, for the purpose of raising funds for its production and operation, issue company bonds in accordance with this Law.

Article 160 Company bonds mentioned in this Law mean negotiable instrument issued by a company in accordance with the legal

程序发行的、约定在一定期限还本付息的有价证券。

第一百六十一条 发行公司债券,必须符合下列条件:

(一)股份有限公司的净资产额不低于人民币三千万元,有限责任公司的净资产额不低于人民币六千万元;

(二)累计债券总额不超过公司净资产额的百分之四十;

(三)最近三年平均可分配利润足以支付公司债券一年的利息;

(四)筹集的资金投向符合国家产业政策;

(五)债券的利率不得超过国务院限定的利率水平;

(六)国务院规定的其他条件。

发行公司债券筹集的资金,必须用于审批机关批准的用途,不得用于弥补亏损和非生产性支出。

第一百六十二条 凡有下列情形之一的,不得再次发行公司债券:

(一)前一次发行的公司债券尚未募足的;

(二)对已发行的公司债券或者其债务有违约或者延迟支付本息的事实,且仍处于继续状态的。

第一百六十三条 股份有限公司、有限责任公司发行

procedures with repayment of the principal and payment of the interest within a definite time limit.

Article 161 To issue company bonds, the following conditions must be met:

(1) for a joint stock limited company, the value of its net asset may not be lower than RMB 30,000,000 yuan; for a limited liability company, the value of its net asset may not be lower than RMB 60,000,000 yuan;

(2) the accumulated value of the bonds issued may not exceed forty percent of the value of the net assets of the company;

(3) the average distributable profits for the past three years shall be sufficient to pay the interest on the company bonds for one year;

(4) the funds to be raised must be invested in accordance with the industrial policies of the State;

(5) the interest rate for the bonds shall not exceed the ceiling fixed by the State Council; and

(6) other conditions as stipulated by the State Council.

Funds raised through the issue of company bonds must be used for the purpose approved by the examination and approval authorities and shall not be used to make up the losses of the company or for non-production expenditure.

Article 162 In any of the following circumstances, a company may not make another issue of bonds:

(1) if the company bonds of the previous issue have not been fully subscribed for; or

(2) if it is a fact that the company has defaulted on, or deferred repayment of the principal and the payment of interest of its previously issued company bonds or its debts, and such default or deferment still persists.

Article 163 For a joint stock limited company and a limited

公司债券,由董事会制订方案,股东会作出决议。

国有独资公司发行公司债券,应由国家授权投资的机构或者国家授权的部门作出决定。

依照前二款规定作出决议或者决定后,公司应当向国务院证券管理部门报请批准。

第一百六十四条 公司债券的发行规模由国务院确定。国务院证券管理部门审批公司债券的发行,不得超过国务院确定的规模。

国务院证券管理部门对符合本法规定的发行公司债券的申请,予以批准;对不符合本法规定的申请,不予批准。

对已作出的批准如发现不符合本法规定的,应予撤销。尚未发行公司债券的,停止发行;已经发行公司债券的,发行的公司应当向认购人退还所缴款项并加算银行同期存款利息。

第一百六十五条 公司向国务院证券管理部门申请批准发行公司债券,应当提交下列文件:

(一)公司登记证明;

liability company to issue company bonds, its board of directors shall formulate a plan therefor, and a pertinent resolution shall be adopted by the shareholders meeting.

For a wholly State-owned company to issue company bonds, a decision on the approval shall be made by the State-authorized investment institution or the department authorized by the State.

Where a resolution or decision is made in accordance with the preceding two paragraphs of this Article, the company shall submit the matter to the department of security administration under the State Council for approval.

Article 164 The scale of the company bond issues shall be determined by the State Council. Issues of company bonds examined and approved by the department of security administration under the State Council shall not exceed the scale determined by the State Council.

The department of security administration under the State Council shall approve the application for issuing company bonds if it conforms with the provisions of this Law and shall disapprove the application if it does not conform with the provisions of this Law.

If an approval that has been granted is found not to be in compliance with the stipulations of this Law, such an approval shall be withdrawn. In the event that company bonds have not yet been issued, the company shall stop issuing the bonds; if the company bond issue has already commenced, the issuing company shall refund the subscribers the money already paid for their subscriptions plus bank deposit interest calculated for the same period of time.

Article 165 Where a company applies to the department of security administration under the State Council for issuing company bonds, the following documents shall be submitted:

(1) the registration certificate of the company;

(二)公司章程;

(三)公司债券募集办法;

(四)资产评估报告和验资报告。

第一百六十六条 发行公司债券的申请经批准后,应当公告公司债券募集办法。

公司债券募集办法中应当载明下列主要事项:

(一)公司名称;

(二)债券总额和债券的票面金额;

(三)债券的利率;

(四)还本付息的期限和方式;

(五)债券发行的起止日期;

(六)公司净资产额;

(七)已发行的尚未到期的公司债券总额;

(八)公司债券的承销机构。

第一百六十七条 公司发行公司债券,必须在债券上载明公司名称、债券票面金额、利率、偿还期限等事项,并由董事长签名,公司盖章。

第一百六十八条 公司债券可分为记名债券和无记名债券。

第一百六十九条 公司发行公司债券应当置备公司债券存根簿。

发行记名公司债券的,应当在公司债券存根簿上载明下列事项:

(一)债券持有人的姓名或者名称及住所;

(2) the articles of association of the company;

(3) the method of offer of the company bonds; and

(4) an asset valuation report and an asset verification report.

Article 166 After an application for the issue of company bonds is approved, the company shall make a public announcement of the method of offer of the company bonds.

The method of offer of company bonds shall specify the following main particulars:

(1) the name of the company;

(2) the total amount of the bonds and their par value;

(3) the interest rate of the bonds;

(4) the time limit for and the method of the repayment of the principal and the payment of interest;

(5) the beginning and ending dates of the bond issue;

(6) the amount of the net assets of the company;

(7) the total amount of the undue bonds issued by the company; and

(8) the selling agency of the company bonds.

Article 167 Company bonds issued by a company must clearly carry thereon items such as the name of the company, the par value, the interest rate and the time limit for repayment, and the bonds shall be signed by the chairman of the board of directors and sealed by the company.

Article 168 Company bonds may be divided into registered bonds and bearer bonds.

Article 169 A company issuing company bonds shall prepare the counterfoils of bonds issued.

When registered company bonds are issued, the counterfoils of bonds shall specify the following:

(1) the name or title and domicile of the bondholder;

(二)债券持有人取得债券的日期及债券的编号;

(三)债券总额,债券的票面金额,债券的利率,债券的还本付息的期限和方式;

(四)债券的发行日期。

发行无记名公司债券的,应当在公司债券存根簿上载明债券总额、利率、偿还期限和方式、发行日期及债券的编号。

第一百七十条 公司债券可以转让。转让公司债券应当在依法设立的证券交易场所进行。

公司债券的转让价格由转让人与受让人约定。

第一百七十一条 记名债券,由债券持有人以背书方式或者法律、行政法规规定的其他方式转让。

记名债券的转让,由公司将受让人的姓名或者名称及住所记载于公司债券存根簿。

无记名债券,由债券持有人在依法设立的证券交易场所将该债券交付给受让人后即发生转让的效力。

第一百七十二条 上市公司经股东大会决议可以发行可转换为股票的公司债券,并在公司债券募集办法中规定具体的转换办法。

(2) the date on which the holder acquired the bonds and their serial numbers;

(3) the total amount of the bonds, the par value, the interest rate of the bonds and the method of and time limit for repayment of the principal and payment of interest; and

(4) the issuing date of the bonds.

Where bearer company bonds are issued, the counterfoils of the company bonds shall specify the total amount of the bonds, the interest rate, the time limit for and method of repayment of the principal and payment of interest, the issuing date of the bonds and the serial numbers.

Article 170 Company bonds may be transferred. The transfer shall be carried out at the securities exchanges established in accordance with the law.

The price for the transfer of the company bonds shall be agreed upon by the transferor and transferee.

Article 171 Registered bonds shall be transferred by means of endorsement by the bondholder or by other means provided for by the law or administrative rules and regulations.

Where registered bonds are transferred, the name and domicile of the transferee shall be recorded in the counterfoils of the company bonds.

Where bearer bonds are transferred, the transfer becomes effective immediately after the bondholder delivers his bonds to the transferee at a securities exchange established in accordance with the law.

Article 172 Upon adoption of a resolution by the shareholders general meeting, a listed company may issue company bonds which can be converted into shares. The specific measures for the conversion shall be stipulated in the method of offer of the company bonds.

发行可转换为股票的公司债券,应当报请国务院证券管理部门批准。公司债券可转换为股票的,除具备发行公司债券的条件外,还应当符合股票发行的条件。

发行可转换为股票的公司债券,应当在债券上标明可转换公司债券字样,并在公司债券存根簿上载明可转换公司债券的数额。

第一百七十三条 发行可转换为股票的公司债券的,公司应当按照其转换办法向债券持有人换发股票,但债券持有人对转换股票或者不转换股票有选择权。

第六章 公司财务、会计

第一百七十四条 公司应当依照法律、行政法规和国务院财政主管部门的规定建立本公司的财务、会计制度。

第一百七十五条 公司应当在每一会计年度终了时制作财务会计报告,并依法经审查验证。

财务会计报告应当包括下列财务会计报表及附属明细表:

(一)资产负债表;

(二)损益表;

(三)财务状况变动表;

The issue of company bonds convertible into shares shall be subjected to the approval of the department of securities administration under the State Council. Company bonds convertible into shares shall, in addition to satisfying the conditions for the issue of company bonds, satisfy the conditions for the issue of shares.

In issuing company bonds convertible into shares, the words "convertible company bonds" shall be clearly indicated on the bonds and the amount of convertible company bonds shall be recorded in the counterfoils of company bonds.

Article 173 A company that issues company bonds convertible into shares shall let the bondholders convert their bonds into shares in accordance with the convertion measures. However, bondholders shall have an option whether or not to convert their bonds into shares.

Chapter VI Financial Affairs and Accounting of Companies

Article 174 A company shall establish its financial and accounting system in accordance with the law, administrative rules and regulations, and the stipulations of the department in charge of financial affairs under the State Council.

Article 175 At the end of each fiscal year, a company shall prepare its financial and accounting report, which shall be examined and verified in accordance with the law.

The financial and accounting report shall include the following financial and accounting statements and annexed detailed schedules:

(1) a balance sheet;

(2) a profit and loss statement;

(3) a statement on changes in the financial position of the

(四)财务情况说明书；

(五)利润分配表。

第一百七十六条 有限责任公司应当按照公司章程规定的期限将财务会计报告送交各股东。

股份有限公司的财务会计报告应当在召开股东大会年会的二十日以前置备于本公司，供股东查阅。

以募集设立方式成立的股份有限公司必须公告其财务会计报告。

第一百七十七条 公司分配当年税后利润时，应当提取利润的百分之十列入公司法定公积金，并提取利润的百分之五至百分之十列入公司法定公益金。公司法定公积金累计额为公司注册资本的百分之五十以上的，可不再提取。

公司的法定公积金不足以弥补上一年度公司亏损的，在依照前款规定提取法定公积金和法定公益金之前，应当先用当年利润弥补亏损。

公司在从税后利润中提取法定公积金后，经股东会决议，可以提取任意公积金。

公司弥补亏损和提取公积金、法定公益金后所余利润，

company;

(4) a statement explaining the financial situation of the company; and

(5) a statement regarding the distribution of profits.

Article 176 A limited liability company shall send the financial and accounting report to each of its shareholders within the time limit stipulated in its articles of association.

A joint stock limited company shall make the financial and accounting report available at the company for examination by its shareholders twenty days prior to the convening of the shareholders annual general meeting.

A joint stock limited company incorporated by means of share offer must announce its financial and accounting report.

Article 177 When a company distributes the annual after-tax profits, it shall allocate ten percent of its profits to its statutory common reserve fund and another five to ten percent to its statutory common welfare fund. Where the accumulated amount of the statutory common reserve fund has exceeded fifty percent of the registered capital of the company, no further allocation may be made.

Where the statutory common reserve fund is insufficient to make up the company's losses of the previous fiscal year, the company shall apply its annual after-tax profits to making up its losses before allocating such profits, in accordance with provisions of the preceding paragraph, to the statutory common reserve fund and statutory common welfare fund.

After making its allocation to the statutory common reserve fund from the company's after-tax profits, the company may, upon resolution made by the shareholders meeting, make allocations to the discretionary common reserve fund.

After a company makes up its losses and makes allocations to the

有限责任公司按照股东的出资比例分配,股份有限公司按照股东持有的股份比例分配。

股东会或者董事会违反前款规定,在公司弥补亏损和提取法定公积金、法定公益金之前向股东分配利润的,必须将违反规定分配的利润退还公司。

第一百七十八条 股份有限公司依照本法规定,以超过股票票面金额的发行价格发行股份所得的溢价款以及国务院财政主管部门规定列入资本公积金的其他收入,应当列为公司资本公积金。

第一百七十九条 公司的公积金用于弥补公司的亏损,扩大公司生产经营或者转为增加公司资本。

股份有限公司经股东大会决议将公积金转为资本时,按股东原有股份比例派送新股或者增加每股面值。但法定公积金转为资本时,所留存的该项公积金不得少于注册资本的百分之二十五。

第一百八十条 公司提取的法定公益金用于本公司职

statutory common reserve fund and the statutory common welfare fund, a limited liability company shall distribute the remaining profits to its shareholders according to the proportion of capital subscribed for by each shareholder, and a joint stock limited company shall distribute the remaining profits to its shareholders according to the proportion of the shareholdings held by each shareholder.

Where the shareholders meeting or the board of directors violates the provisions of the preceding paragraphs by distributing profits to the shareholders before making up the company's losses and making allocations to the statutory common reserve fund and the statutory common welfare fund, the profits distributed in violation of the legal provisions must be returned to the company.

Article 178 The premium income derived from issuing shares above par by a joint stock limited company in accordance with the provisions of this Law, and other income which according to the rules set by the departments in charge of financial affairs under the State Council should be entered into the capital common reserve fund, shall be entered into the capital common reserve fund of the company.

Article 179 A company's common reserve fund shall be used to make up the company's losses, to expand the production and operation of the company or to increase the capital of the company by means of conversion.

If a joint stock limited company converts its common reserve fund into capital upon a resolution made by the shareholders general meeting, it shall issue new shares in proportion to the original shares held by the shareholders or increase the original par value of each share. However, when the statutory common reserve fund is converted into its capital, the remaining amount of the statutory common reserve fund shall not be less than twenty five percent of the registered capital.

Article 180 The statutory common welfare fund retained by a

工的集体福利。

第一百八十一条 公司除法定的会计帐册外,不得另立会计帐册。

对公司资产,不得以任何个人名义开立帐户存储。

第七章 公司合并、分立

第一百八十二条 公司合并或者分立,应当由公司的股东会作出决议。

第一百八十三条 股份有限公司合并或者分立,必须经国务院授权的部门或者省级人民政府批准。

第一百八十四条 公司合并可以采取吸收合并和新设合并两种形式。

一个公司吸收其他公司为吸收合并,被吸收的公司解散。二个以上公司合并设立一个新的公司为新设合并,合并各方解散。

公司合并,应当由合并各方签订合并协议,并编制资产负债表及财产清单。公司应当自作出合并决议之日起十日内通知债权人,并于三十日内在报纸上至少公告三次。债权人自接到通知书之日起三十日内,未接到通知书的自第

company shall be used for the collective welfare of the company's staff and workers.

Article 181 A company shall not have any other account books in addition to its statutory account books.

No account may be opened in the name of any individual for deposit of a company's assets.

Chapter VII Merger and Division of Companies

Article 182 The merger or division of a company shall require the adoption of a resolution by its shareholders meeting of the company.

Article 183 The merger or division of a joint stock limited company must be approved by the department authorized by the State Council or by the people's government at the provincial level.

Article 184 The merger of a company may take the form of merger by absorption or merger by new establishment.

When a company absorbs another, it is an absorption merger, and the company being absorbed shall be dissolved. When two or more companies merge to establish a new company, it is merger for new establishment, and all parties being merged shall be dissolved.

When companies merge, the parties to a merger shall sign a merger agreement and formulate a balance sheet and a detailed inventory of assets. The company shall inform its creditors of the intended merger within ten days following the date on which the merger resolution is adopted, and make at least three announcements in newspaper within thirty days. The creditors shall have the right to claim full repayment of their debts or provision of a corresponding guarantee from the company within thirty days from the date of receipt

一次公告之日起九十日内,有权要求公司清偿债务或者提供相应的担保。不清偿债务或者不提供相应的担保的,公司不得合并。

公司合并时,合并各方的债权、债务,应当由合并后存续的公司或者新设的公司承继。

第一百八十五条 公司分立,其财产作相应的分割。

公司分立时,应当编制资产负债表及财产清单。公司应当自作出分立决议之日起十日内通知债权人,并于三十日内在报纸上至少公告三次。债权人自接到通知书之日起三十日内,未接到通知书的自第一次公告之日起九十日内,有权要求公司清偿债务或者提供相应的担保。不清偿债务或者不提供相应的担保的,公司不得分立。

公司分立前的债务按所达成的协议由分立后的公司承担。

第一百八十六条 公司需要减少注册资本时,必须编制资产负债表及财产清单。

公司应当自作出减少注册资本决议之日起十日内通知债权人,并于三十日内在报纸上至少公告三次。债权人自接到通知书之日起三十日内,未接到通知书的自第一次公告之日起九十日内,有权要求公司清偿债务或者提供相应的担保。

of the notice or, within ninety days from the date of the first public announcement for those who have not received the notice. The company that fails to repay its debts in full or to provide a corresponding guarantee shall not be merged.

The claims and debts of the parties to a merger shall be succeeded to by the absorbing company or the newly established company when companies are merged.

Article 185 Where a company proceeds into a division, its assets shall be divided correspondingly.

Where a company decides to divide itself, it shall formulate a balance sheet and a detailed inventory of assets and shall inform its creditors of the intended division within ten days following the date on which the division resolution is adopted, and make at least three announcements in newspaper within thirty days. The creditors shall have the right to claim full repayment of their debts or provision of a corresponding guarantee from the company within thirty days from the date of receipt of the notice or, within ninety days from the date of the first public announcement for those who have not received the notice. The company that fails to pay its debts in full or to provide a corresponding guarantee shall not be divided.

The debts prior to the division of a company shall be assumed by the companies following the division in accordance with the agreement reached between them.

Article 186 Where a company intends to reduce its registered capital, it must formulate a balance sheet and a detailed inventory of assets.

The company shall inform its creditors of the planned reduction of its registered capital within ten days following the date on which the resolution to reduce its capital is adopted, and make at least three announcements in newspaper within thirty days following the a

公司减少资本后的注册资本不得低于法定的最低限额。

第一百八十七条 有限责任公司增加注册资本时,股东认缴新增资本的出资,按照本法设立有限责任公司缴纳出资的有关规定执行。

股份有限公司为增加注册资本发行新股时,股东认购新股应当按照本法设立股份有限公司缴纳股款的有关规定执行。

第一百八十八条 公司合并或者分立,登记事项发生变更的,应当依法向公司登记机关办理变更登记;公司解散的,应当依法办理公司注销登记;设立新公司的,应当依法办理公司设立登记。

公司增加或者减少注册资本,应当依法向公司登记机关办理变更登记。

foresaid date. The creditors shall have the right to claim full repayment of their debts or provision of a corresponding guarantee from the company within thirty days from the date of the receipt of the notice or, within ninety days from the date of the first public announcement for those who have not received the notice.

After the reduction of capital, the amount of a company's registered capital shall not be lower than the statutory minimum.

Article 187 Where a limited liability company increases its registered capital, the capital contributions to the newly increased shares subscribed for by the shareholders shall be governed by the relevant provisions of this Law regarding the subscription for capital contributions in connection with the incorporation of a limited liability company.

Where a joint stock limited company issues new shares to increase its registered capital, shareholders shall subscribe for the new shares in accordance with the relevant provisions of this Law regarding the payment of subscription money in connection with the incorporation of a joint stock limited company.

Article 188 Where the merger or division of a company involves changes in registered items, such changes shall be registered according to law with the Company Registration Authority. Where a company is dissolved, it shall apply for cancellation of its registration in accordance with the law. Where a new company is incorporated, the registration of the incorporation of the company shall be carried out according to law.

Where a company increases or reduces its registered capital, it shall apply to the Company Registration Authority for registration of the changes in accordance with the law.

第八章　公司破产、解散和清算

第一百八十九条　公司因不能清偿到期债务,被依法宣告破产的,由人民法院依照有关法律的规定,组织股东、有关机关及有关专业人员成立清算组,对公司进行破产清算。

第一百九十条　公司有下列情形之一的,可以解散:

(一)公司章程规定的营业期限届满或者公司章程规定的其他解散事由出现时;

(二)股东会决议解散;

(三)因公司合并或者分立需要解散的。

第一百九十一条　公司依照前条第(一)项、第(二)项规定解散的,应当在十五日内成立清算组,有限责任公司的清算组由股东组成,股份有限公司的清算组由股东大会确定其人选;逾期不成立清算组进行清算的,债权人可以申请人民法院指定有关人员组成清算组,进行清算。人民法院应当受理该申请,并及时指定清算组成员,进行清算。

第一百九十二条　公司违反法律、行政法规被依法责

Chapter VIII Bankruptcy, Dissolution and Liquidation of Companies

Article 189 Where a company is declared bankrupt according to law because it is unable to pay off its due debts, a people's court shall, in accordance with relevant laws, organize the shareholders, the relevant departments and relevant professionals to form a liquidation committee which shall conduct bankruptcy liquidation of the company.

Article 190 Where one of the following circumstances occurs, a company may be dissolved:

(1) the term of operation as stipulated by the articles of association of the company expires or other reasons for dissolution as stipulated by the articles of association occur;

(2) the shareholders meeting resolves to dissolve the company; or

(3) dissolution is necessary as a result of the merger or division of the company.

Article 191 Where a company is dissolved in accordance with the provisions of item (1) or (2) of the preceding Article, a liquidation committee shall be formed within fifteen days thereafter. A liquidation committee of a limited liability company shall be composed of its shareholders. Membership of a liquidation committee of a joint stock limited company shall be decided upon by its shareholders general meeting. Where a company fails to form a liquidation committee to conduct liquidation within the time limit, its creditors may request a people's court to designate relevant personnel to form a liquidation committee and conduct liquidation. The people's court shall accept such request and without delay designate the members of the liquidation committee to conduct liquidation.

Article 192 Where a company is ordered to be closed down in

令关闭的,应当解散,由有关主管机关组织股东、有关机关及有关专业人员成立清算组,进行清算。

第一百九十三条 清算组在清算期间行使下列职权:

(一)清理公司财产,分别编制资产负债表和财产清单;

(二)通知或者公告债权人;

(三)处理与清算有关的公司未了结的业务;

(四)清缴所欠税款;

(五)清理债权、债务;

(六)处理公司清偿债务后的剩余财产;

(七)代表公司参与民事诉讼活动。

第一百九十四条 清算组应当自成立之日起十日内通知债权人,并于六十日内在报纸上至少公告三次。债权人应当自接到通知书之日起三十日内,未接到通知书的自第一次公告之日起九十日内,向清算组申报其债权。

债权人申报其债权,应当说明债权的有关事项,并提供证明材料。清算组应当对债权进行登记。

第一百九十五条 清算组在清理公司财产、编制资产

accordance with the law due to its violation of the law or administrative rules and regulations, it shall be dissolved. In such a case, the department in charge shall organize the shareholders, relevant departments and relevant professionals to form a liquidation committee to conduct liquidation.

Article 193 During liquidation, a liquidation committee shall exercise the following functions and powers:

(1) to check up on the company's assets, and separately formulate a balance sheet and a detailed inventory of assets;

(2) to notify creditors by notice or announcement;

(3) to dispose of and liquidate the company's unfinished business;

(4) to pay off taxes owed by the company;

(5) to clear up claims and debts;

(6) to dispose of, after paying off the debts of the company, its remaining property; and

(7) to participate in civil lawsuits on behalf of the company.

Article 194 A liquidation committee shall inform the creditors of the company of its establishment within ten days following the date of its establishment, and make at least three announcements in newspaper within sixty days following the aforesaid date. The creditors shall declare their claims to the liquidation committee within thirty days from the date of receipt of the notice or, within ninety days from the date of the first public announcement for those who have not received the notice.

When declaring his claims, a creditor shall specify the relevant items of the claim and provide supporting material. The liquidation committee shall register the claims.

Article 195 After the liquidation committee has checked up on the company's assets, formulated the balance sheet and a detailed inventory of assets, it shall formulate a liquidation plan and shall

负债表和财产清单后,应当制定清算方案,并报股东会或者有关主管机关确认。

公司财产能够清偿公司债务的,分别支付清算费用、职工工资和劳动保险费用,缴纳所欠税款,清偿公司债务。

公司财产按前款规定清偿后的剩余财产,有限责任公司按照股东的出资比例分配,股份有限公司按照股东持有的股份比例分配。

清算期间,公司不得开展新的经营活动。公司财产在未按第二款的规定清偿前,不得分配给股东。

第一百九十六条　因公司解散而清算,清算组在清理公司财产、编制资产负债表和财产清单后,发现公司财产不足清偿债务的,应当立即向人民法院申请宣告破产。

公司经人民法院裁定宣告破产后,清算组应当将清算事务移交给人民法院。

第一百九十七条　公司清算结束后,清算组应当制作清算报告,报股东会或者有关主管机关确认,并报送公司登

submit such plan to the shareholders meeting or the department in charge for confirmation.

Where the assets of the company are sufficient to pay off the company's debts, such assets shall be applied to payment of the liquidation fee, the wages and labour insurance premiums of the staff and workers of the company, due taxes and the company's debts.

The remaining assets of a company after paying off all the debts and expenses as prescribed by the preceding paragraph shall be distributed, in the case of a limited liability company, in proportion to the shareholders capital contributions and, in the case of a joint stock limited company, in proportion to the shareholders shareholdings.

During liquidation, a company may not engage in new business activities. No assets of the company shall be distributed to the shareholders prior to full payments prescribed by the second paragraph of this Article.

Article 196 If a company is liquidated due to its dissolution and the liquidation committee, having checked up on the company's assets and formulated the balance sheet and a detailed inventory of assets, discovers that there are insufficient assets in the company to pay off its debts, the committee shall apply to the people's court for a declaration of bankruptcy of the company.

After the people's court has ruled to declare the company bankrupt, the liquidation committee shall turn the liquidation matters over to the court.

Article 197 After the completion of liquidation, the liquidation committee shall formulate a liquidation report and submit the report to the shareholders meeting or to the department in charge for confirmation and submit it to the Company Registration Authority in order to cancel the registration of the company and publicly announce the company's termination. If no application is made for cancellation

记机关,申请注销公司登记,公告公司终止。不申请注销公司登记的,由公司登记机关吊销其公司营业执照,并予以公告。

第一百九十八条 清算组成员应当忠于职守,依法履行清算义务。

清算组成员不得利用职权收受贿赂或者其他非法收入,不得侵占公司财产。

清算组成员因故意或者重大过失给公司或者债权人造成损失的,应当承担赔偿责任。

第九章　外国公司的分支机构

第一百九十九条 外国公司依照本法规定可以在中国境内设立分支机构,从事生产经营活动。

本法所称外国公司是指依照外国法律在中国境外登记成立的公司。

第二百条 外国公司在中国境内设立分支机构,必须向中国主管机关提出申请,并提交其公司章程、所属国的公司登记证书等有关文件,经批准后,向公司登记机关依法办理登记,领取营业执照。

外国公司分支机构的审批办法由国务院另行规定。

of the company's registration, the Company Registration Authority shall revoke the business licence of the company and publicly announce the revocation.

Article 198 Members of a liquidation committee shall be devoted to their duties and perform their liquidation obligations in accordance with the law.

Members of a liquidation committee shall not accept bribes or other illegal income, or misappropriate the property of the company by taking advantage of their position and power.

Members of a liquidation committee who cause losses to the company or to its creditors, either willfully or through gross negligence, shall be liable for compensation.

Chapter IX   Branches of Foreign Companies

Article 199 A foreign company may, in accordance with this Law, establish a branch within the territory of the People's Republic of China to engage in production and business activities.

A foreign company mentioned in this Law means a company registered and incorporated outside the territory of the People's Republic of China in accordance with foreign laws.

Article 200 A foreign company that intends to establish a branch within the territory of the People's Republic of China must submit an application to the authorities in charge in China together with relevant documents such as its articles of association and the company's registration certificate issued by its country. Upon approval, it shall apply to the Company Registration Authority for registration and for a business licence for the branch according to law.

Measures for examining and approving the establishment of branches of foreign companies shall be formulated separately by the

第二百零一条 外国公司在中国境内设立分支机构,必须在中国境内指定负责该分支机构的代表人或者代理人,并向该分支机构拨付与其所从事的经营活动相适应的资金。

对外国公司分支机构的经营资金需要规定最低限额的,由国务院另行规定。

第二百零二条 外国公司的分支机构应当在其名称中标明该外国公司的国籍及责任形式。

外国公司的分支机构应当在本机构中置备该外国公司章程。

第二百零三条 外国公司属于外国法人,其在中国境内设立的分支机构不具有中国法人资格。

外国公司对其分支机构在中国境内进行经营活动承担民事责任。

第二百零四条 经批准设立的外国公司分支机构,在中国境内从事业务活动,必须遵守中国的法律,不得损害中国的社会公共利益,其合法权益受中国法律保护。

第二百零五条 外国公司撤销其在中国境内的分支机构时,必须依法清偿债务,按照本法有关公司清算程序的规

State Council.

Article 201 A foreign company that establishes a branch within the territory of the People's Republic of China must appoint its representative or agent within the territory of the People's Republic of China to take charge of the branch and shall allocate to the branch funds commensurate with the business which it is to engage in.

Where a minimum amount of operational funds is required for a branch of a foreign company, the State Council shall separately prescribe to that effect.

Article 202 A branch of a foreign company shall clearly indicate in its name the nationality and the form of liability of such foreign company.

The branch shall keep at its domicile a copy of the articles of association of such foreign company.

Article 203 A foreign company is a foreign legal person, so its branch established within the territory of the People's Republic of China shall not have the status of a Chinese legal person in China.

A foreign company shall bear civil liability for the operational activities engaged by its branch within the territory of the People's Republic of China.

Article 204 The business activities engaged in within the territory of the People's Republic of China by branches of foreign companies established upon due approval must comply with the laws of China and shall not harm the social and public interest of China. The lawful rights and interests of such branches shall be protected by the laws of China.

Article 205 Where a foreign company dissolves its branch established within the territory of the People's Republic of China, it must pay off the branch's debts according to law and carry out liquidation in accordance with the relevant procedures concerning

定进行清算。未清偿债务之前,不得将其分支机构的财产移至中国境外。

第十章 法律责任

第二百零六条 违反本法规定,办理公司登记时虚报注册资本、提交虚假证明文件或者采取其他欺诈手段隐瞒重要事实取得公司登记的,责令改正,对虚报注册资本的公司,处以虚报注册资本金额百分之五以上百分之十以下的罚款;对提交虚假证明文件或者采取其他欺诈手段隐瞒重要事实的公司,处以一万元以上十万元以下的罚款;情节严重的,撤销公司登记。构成犯罪的,依法追究刑事责任。

第二百零七条 制作虚假的招股说明书、认股书、公司债券募集办法发行股票或者公司债券的,责令停止发行,退还所募资金及其利息,处以非法募集资金金额百分之一以上百分之五以下的罚款。构成犯罪的,依法追究刑事责任。

第二百零八条 公司的发起人、股东未交付货币、实物或者未转移财产权,虚假出资,欺骗债权人和社会公众的,

company liquidation provided for in this Law. The assets of the branch shall not be transferred out of the territory of the People's Republic of China prior to the full payment of its debts.

Chapter X Legal Liability

Article 206 Where a company obtains its registration by making a false report on its registered capital, submitting falsified certificates, or resorting to other fraudulent means to conceal important facts in violation of this Law when carrying out company registration, it shall be ordered to make a rectification; where a company makes a false report on its registered capital, it shall be fined an amount of not less than five percent but not more than ten percent of the registered capital falsely reported; where a company submits falsified certificates or resorts to other fraudulent means to conceal important facts, it shall be punished with a fine of not less than RMB 10,000 yuan but not more than RMB 100,000 yuan. If the circumstances are serious, the registration of the company shall be revoked. If the case constitutes a crime, criminal liabilities shall be investigated in accordance with the law.

Article 207 Where a company issues shares or company bonds by making false prospectus on share offer, false subscription forms or false methods of offer of company bonds, it shall be ordered to stop the issuance and to refund the funds it has raised and the interest therefrom to the subscribers, and shall be punished with a fine of not less than one percent but not more than five percent of the funds illegally raised. If the case constitutes a crime, criminal liabilities shall be investigated in accordance with the law.

Article 208 Where a sponsor or a shareholder makes a false capital contribution by failing to pay the promised cash or tangible assets, or to

责令改正,处以虚假出资金额百分之五以上百分之十以下的罚款。构成犯罪的,依法追究刑事责任。

第二百零九条 公司的发起人、股东在公司成立后,抽逃其出资的,责令改正,处以所抽逃出资金额百分之五以上百分之十以下的罚款。构成犯罪的,依法追究刑事责任。

第二百一十条 未经本法规定的有关主管部门的批准,擅自发行股票或者公司债券的,责令停止发行,退还所募资金及其利息,处以非法所募资金金额百分之一以上百分之五以下的罚款。构成犯罪的,依法追究刑事责任。

第二百一十一条 公司违反本法规定,在法定的会计帐册以外另立会计帐册的,责令改正,处以一万元以上十万元以下的罚款。构成犯罪的,依法追究刑事责任。

将公司资产以任何个人名义开立帐户存储的,没收违法所得,并处以违法所得一倍以上五倍以下的罚款。构成犯罪的,依法追究刑事责任。

transfer property rights, thereby deceiving the creditors and the general public, he shall be ordered to make a rectification and imposed a fine of not less than five percent but not more than ten percent of the false capital contributions. If the case constitutes a crime, criminal liabilities shall be investigated in accordance with the law.

Article 209 Where a sponsor or a shareholder of a company surreptitiously withdraws his capital contribution after the incorporation of the company, rectification shall be ordered and a fine of not less than five percent but not more than ten percent of the amount of capital contribution surreptitiously withdrawn shall be imposed. If the case constitutes a crime, criminal liabilities shall be investigated in accordance with the law.

Article 210 Where a company issues shares or company bonds without the approval of the relevant department in charge as stipulated by this Law, it shall be ordered to stop the issuance and to refund the funds it has raised with interest, and a fine of not less than one percent but not more than five percent of the funds illegally raised shall be imposed. If the case constitutes a crime, criminal liabilities shall be investigated in accordance with the law.

Article 211 Where a company violates the provisions of this Law by setting up account books in addition to its statutory account books, it shall be ordered to make a rectification and imposed a fine of not less than RMB10,000 yuan but not more than RMB100,000 yuan. If the case constitutes a crime, criminal liabilities shall be investigated in accordance with the law.

Whoever deposits the assets of a company in a personal account shall be confiscated of the illegal gains and imposed upon a fine from one to five times the amount of the illegal gains. If the case constitutes a crime, criminal liabilities shall be investigated in accordance with the law.

第二百一十二条　公司向股东和社会公众提供虚假的或者隐瞒重要事实的财务会计报告的,对直接负责的主管人员和其他直接责任人员处以一万元以上十万元以下的罚款。构成犯罪的,依法追究刑事责任。

　　第二百一十三条　违反本法规定,将国有资产低价折股、低价出售或者无偿分给个人的,对直接负责的主管人员和其他直接责任人员依法给予行政处分。构成犯罪的,依法追究刑事责任。

　　第二百一十四条　董事、监事、经理利用职权收受贿赂、其他非法收入或者侵占公司财产的,没收违法所得,责令退还公司财产,由公司给予处分。构成犯罪的,依法追究刑事责任。

　　董事、经理挪用公司资金或者将公司资金借贷给他人的,责令退还公司的资金,由公司给予处分,将其所得收入归公司所有。构成犯罪的,依法追究刑事责任。

　　董事、经理违反本法规定,以公司资产为本公司的股东或者其他个人债务提供担保的,责令取消担保,并依法承担

Article 212 Where a company submits to the shareholders and the general public false financial and accounting reports or reports concealing important facts, the persons in charge and other persons held directly responsible shall be imposed upon a fine of not less than RMB10,000 yuan but not more than RMB 100,000 yuan. If the case constitutes a crime, criminal liabilities shall be investigated in accordance with the law.

Article 213 Where this Law is violated by converting the State-owned assets into shares at a depressed value, or selling them at low prices, or distributing them gratuitously to individuals, the persons in charge and other persons held directly responsible shall be given administrative sanctions in accordance with the law. If the case constitutes a crime, criminal liabilities shall be investigated in accordance with the law.

Article 214 Where a director, a supervisor or the manager of a company takes advantage of his position and powers to accept bribes, to take other illegal gains or to misappropriate company property, he shall be confiscated of the illegal gains, ordered to return such property to the company, and imposed upon a sanction. If the case constitutes a crime, criminal liabilities shall be investigated in accordance with the law.

Where a director or the manager misappropriates company funds or lends company funds to another person, he shall be ordered to return such funds to the company; the gains derived therefrom shall belong to the company; the company shall impose a sanction upon him. If the case constitutes a crime, criminal liabilities shall be investigated in accordance with the law.

Where a director or the manager violates the provisions of this Law by providing company assets as a guarantee for personal debts of a shareholder of its company or of another person, he shall be ordered to

赔偿责任,将违法提供担保取得的收入归公司所有。情节严重的,由公司给予处分。

第二百一十五条　董事、经理违反本法规定自营或者为他人经营与其所任职公司同类的营业的,除将其所得收入归公司所有外,并可由公司给予处分。

第二百一十六条　公司不按照本法规定提取法定公积金、法定公益金的,责令如数补足应当提取的金额,并可对公司处以一万元以上十万元以下的罚款。

第二百一十七条　公司在合并、分立、减少注册资本或者进行清算时,不按照本法规定通知或者公告债权人的,责令改正,对公司处以一万元以上十万元以下的罚款。

公司在进行清算时,隐匿财产,对资产负债表或者财产清单作虚伪记载或者未清偿债务前分配公司财产的,责令改正,对公司处以隐匿财产或者未清偿债务前分配公司财产金额百分之一以上百分之五以下的罚款。对直接负责的主管人员和其他直接责任人员处以一万元以上十万元以下的罚款。构成犯罪的,依法追究刑事责任。

cancel the guarantee and shall be liable for compensation in accordance with the law; the gains derived from the illegal provision of guarantee shall belong to the company. If the circumstances are serious, the company shall impose a sanction upon him.

Article 215 Where a director or the manager violates the provisions of this Law by engaging for his own account or for another person in the same kind of business as his company is engaged in, the income derived therefrom shall belong to the company. In addition, the company may impose a sanction upon him.

Article 216 Where a company fails to make allocations to its statutory common reserve fund or statutory common welfare fund in accordance with this Law, the company shall be ordered to make up the amount that it is required to allocate and shall be imposed upon a fine of not less than RMB10,000 yuan but not more than RMB100,000 yuan.

Article 217 Where a company fails to issue a notice or make an announcement to its creditors according to this Law in case of merger, division, reduction of its registered capital or liquidation, it shall be ordered to make a rectification and be imposed upon a fine of not less than RMB10,000 yuan but not more than RMB 100,000 yuan.

Where a company, in the process of its liquidation, conceals property, records false information in its balance sheet or inventory of assets or, distributes the company assets prior to the full payment of its debts, it shall be ordered to make a rectification and be imposed upon a fine of not less than one percent but not more than five percent of the amount concealed or of the amount distributed prior to the full payment of the debts of the company. The persons in charge and others held directly responsible shall be imposed upon a fine of not less than RMB 10,000 yuan but not more than RMB100,000 yuan. If the case constitutes a crime, criminal liabilities shall be investigated in

第二百一十八条　清算组不按照本法规定向公司登记机关报送清算报告,或者报送清算报告隐瞒重要事实或者有重大遗漏的,责令改正。

清算组成员利用职权徇私舞弊、谋取非法收入或者侵占公司财产的,责令退还公司财产,没收违法所得,并可处以违法所得一倍以上五倍以下的罚款。构成犯罪的,依法追究刑事责任。

第二百一十九条　承担资产评估、验资或者验证的机构提供虚假证明文件的,没收违法所得,处以违法所得一倍以上五倍以下的罚款,并可由有关主管部门依法责令该机构停业,吊销直接责任人员的资格证书。构成犯罪的,依法追究刑事责任。

承担资产评估、验资或者验证的机构因过失提供有重大遗漏的报告的,责令改正,情节较重的,处以所得收入一倍以上三倍以下的罚款,并可由有关主管部门依法责令该机构停业,吊销直接责任人员的资格证书。

accordance with the law.

Article 218 Where a liquidation committee fails to submit a liquidation report to the Company Registration Authority in accordance with the provisions of this Law, or where a report submitted conceals major facts or contains major omissions, it shall be ordered to make a rectification.

Where a member of the liquidation committee takes advantage of his position and power to practise favoritism for personal gains, seek illegal income or misappropriate the property of the company, he shall be ordered to return the property to the company, confiscated of his illegal gains and imposed upon a fine from one to five times the amount of his illegal gains. If the case constitutes a crime, criminal liabilities shall be investigated in accordance with the law.

Article 219 Where an institution in charge of asset valuation, capital verification or certificate verification provides false documents of certification, the illegal income derived therefrom shall be confiscated and a fine from one to five times the amount of the illegal income shall be imposed; the relevant department in charge may order the institution to suspend its business and revoke the qualification certificates of those held directly responsible according to law. If the case constitutes a crime, criminal liabilities shall be investigated in accordance with the law.

Where an institution in charge of asset valuation, capital verification or certificate verification provides by negligence reports with major omissions, it shall be ordered to make a rectification; where the circumstances are serious, a fine from one to three times the amount of the income derived therefrom shall be imposed, and the relevant department in charge may order the institution to suspend its business and revoke the qualification certificates of those held directly responsible according to law.

第二百二十条 国务院授权的有关主管部门,对不符合本法规定条件的设立公司的申请予以批准,或者对不符合本法规定条件的股份发行的申请予以批准,情节严重的,对直接负责的主管人员和其他直接责任人员,依法给予行政处分。构成犯罪的,依法追究刑事责任。

第二百二十一条 国务院证券管理部门对不符合本法规定条件的募集股份、股票上市和债券发行的申请予以批准,情节严重的,对直接负责的主管人员和其他直接责任人员,依法给予行政处分。构成犯罪的,依法追究刑事责任。

第二百二十二条 公司登记机关对不符合本法规定条件的登记申请予以登记,情节严重的,对直接负责的主管人员和其他直接责任人员,依法给予行政处分。构成犯罪的,依法追究刑事责任。

第二百二十三条 公司登记机关的上级部门强令公司登记机关对不符合本法规定条件的登记申请予以登记的,或者对违法登记进行包庇的,对直接负责的主管人员和其他直接责任人员依法给予行政处分。构成犯罪的,依法追究刑事责任。

Article 220 Where a relevant department in charge authorized by the State Council approves an application for the incorporation of a company or an application for the issue of shares that does not satisfy the conditions as stipulated in this Law, if the circumstances are serious, the persons in charge and others held directly responsible shall be given administrative sanctions according to law. If the case constitutes a crime, criminal liabilities shall be investigated in accordance with the law.

Article 221 Where the department of security administration under the State Council approves an application for the offer of shares, the listing of shares or the issue of bonds that does not satisfy the conditions as stipulated in this Law, if the circumstances are serious, the persons in charge and others held directly responsible shall be given administrative sanctions according to law. If the case constitutes a crime, criminal liabilities shall be investigated in accordance with the law.

Article 222 Where the Company Registration Authority approves an application for registration which does not meet the requirements as stipulated in this Law, if the circumstances are serious, the persons in charge and others held directly responsible shall be given administrative sanctions according to law. If the case constitutes a crime, criminal liabilities shall be investigated in accordance with the law.

Article 223 Where departments at a level higher than the Company Registration Authority force the Company Registration Authority to approve an application for registration which does not meet the requirements as stipulated in this Law or, covers up an illegal registration, the persons in charge and others held directly responsible shall be given administrative sanctions according to law. If the case constitutes a crime, criminal liabilities shall be investigated in accordance with the law.

第二百二十四条 未依法登记为有限责任公司或者股份有限公司,而冒用有限责任公司或者股份有限公司名义的,责令改正或者予以取缔,并可处以一万元以上十万元以下的罚款。构成犯罪的,依法追究刑事责任。

第二百二十五条 公司成立后无正当理由超过六个月未开业的,或者开业后自行停业连续六个月以上的,由公司登记机关吊销其公司营业执照。

公司登记事项发生变更时,未按照本法规定办理有关变更登记的,责令限期登记,逾期不登记的,处以一万元以上十万元以下的罚款。

第二百二十六条 外国公司违反本法规定,擅自在中国境内设立分支机构的,责令改正或者关闭,并可处以一万元以上十万元以下的罚款。

第二百二十七条 依照本法履行审批职责的有关主管部门,对符合法定条件的申请,不予批准的,或者公司登记机关对符合法定条件的申请,不予登记的,当事人可以依法

Article 224 Where a company that has not registered according to law as a limited liability company or a joint stock limited company assumes the name of "limited liability company" or "joint stock limited company", it shall be ordered to make a rectification or be banned, and a fine of not less than RMB 10,000 yuan but not more than RMB 100,000 yuan may be imposed. If the case constitutes a crime, criminal liabilities shall be investigated in accordance with the law.

Article 225 Where a company fails to commence its business without justification within the period of more than six months of its incorporation or, after commencing its business, suspends business at its own will for a period of six consecutive months or more, the Company Registration Authority shall revoke the company's business licence.

Where a company fails to apply for modification registration in accordance with the provisions of this Law whenever modification occurs in items of company registration, it shall be ordered to conduct modification registration within a specified time limit; and if the company still fails to register within the specified time limit, a fine of not less than RMB10,000 yuan but not more than RMB 100,000 yuan shall be imposed.

Article 226 Where a foreign company, in violation of the provisions of this Law, establishes a branch within the territory of the People's Republic of China without authorization, it shall be ordered to make a rectification or to be closed down, and a fine of not less than RMB10,000 yuan but not more than RMB 100,000 yuan may be imposed.

Article 227 Where a relevant department in charge performing examination and approval duties according to this Law refuses to approve an application which meets the statutory requirements or the Company Registration Authority refuses an application for registration which meets the statutory requirements, the party concerned may

申请复议或者提起行政诉讼。

第二百二十八条 公司违反本法规定,应当承担民事赔偿责任和缴纳罚款、罚金的,其财产不足以支付时,先承担民事赔偿责任。

第十一章 附　　则

第二百二十九条 本法施行前依照法律、行政法规、地方性法规和国务院有关主管部门制定的《有限责任公司规范意见》、《股份有限公司规范意见》登记成立的公司,继续保留,其中不完全具备本法规定的条件的,应当在规定的限期内达到本法规定的条件。具体实施办法,由国务院另行规定。

属于高新技术的股份有限公司,发起人以工业产权和非专利技术作价出资的金额占公司注册资本的比例,公司发行新股、申请股票上市的条件,由国务院另行规定。

第二百三十条 本法自1994年7月1日起施行。

apply for reconsideration or institute an administrative lawsuit in accordance with the law.

Article 228 Where a company violating the provisions of this Law should assume civil liability for compensation and pay fines and penalties, and the company's property is insufficient to pay such compensation, fines and penalties, the company shall assume the civil liability for compensation first.

Chapter XI Supplementary Provisions

Article 229 Companies registered and incorporated in accordance with the law, administrative rules and regulations, local regulations or the Opinions on Standardization of Limited Liability Companies and the Opinions on Standardization of Joint Stock Limited Companies formulated by the relevant competent departments under the State Council prior to the implementation of this Law shall continue to be retained; companies which do not fully meet the requirements as stipulated in this Law shall meet all such requirements within a prescribed time limit. Specific measures for the implementation thereof shall be formulated separately by the State Council.

With regard to a new and high-tech joint stock limited company, the proportion of the investment, made by a promoter in the form of industrial property rights and non-patent technology at their appraised value, in the registered capital of the company, the requirements the company must meet in order to issue new shares or apply to have the shares listed shall be separately formulated by the State Council.

Article 230 This Law shall go into effect as of July 1, 1994.

英文及中英文对照法律文本系列
Series of Laws in Chinese-English/English Edition

序号	书　　名 (Titles)	定价 (Prices) (元)
1	中华人民共和国刑法 (中英对照) Criminal Law (Chinese-English)	25.00
2	中华人民共和国民法通则、民事诉讼法 (中英对照) General Principles of the Civil Law and Civil Procedure Law (Chinese-English)	15.00
3	中华人民共和国海商法、海事诉讼特别程序法 (中英对照) Maritime Code and Special Maritime Procedure Law (Chinese-English)	15.00
4	中华人民共和国刑事诉讼法 (中英对照) Criminal Procedure Law (Chinese-English)	15.00
5	中华人民共和国专利法、商标法、著作权法 (中英对照) Patent Law, Trademark Law and Copyright Law (Chinese-English)	15.00
6	中华人民共和国合同法 (中英对照) Contract Law (Chinese-English)	12.00
7	中华人民共和国公司法 (中英对照) Company Law (Chinese-English)	12.00
8	中华人民共和国证券法 (中英对照) Securities Law (Chinese-English)	9.00
9	中华人民共和国工会法 (中英对照) Trade Union Law (Chinese-English)	8.00
10	中华人民共和国海关法 (中英对照) Customs Law (Chinese-English)	8.00
11	中华人民共和国个人所得税法、税收征管法 (中英对照) Individual Income Tax Law and Law on Administration Tax Collection (Chinese-English)	8.00
12	中华人民共和国行政诉讼法、行政复议法 (中英对照) Administrative Procedure Law and Administrative Reconsideration Law (Chinese-English)	8.00

序号	书 名(Titles)	定价(Prices)(元)
13	中华人民共和国行政处罚法、行政监察法(中英对照) Administrative Penalty Law and Administrative Supervision Law (Chinese-English)	8.00
14	中华人民共和国乡镇企业法、合伙企业法、个人独资企业法(中英对照) Township Enterprises Law, Partnership Enterprises Law and Individual Proprietorship Enterprises Law (Chinese-English)	8.00
15	中华人民共和国外资企业法、中外合作经营企业法、中外合资经营企业法(中英对照) Foreign-Capital Enterprise Law, Chinese-Foreign Contractual Joint Ventures Law and Chinese-Foreign Equity Joint Ventures Law (Chinese-English)	6.00
16	中华人民共和国执业医师法、药品管理法(中英对照) Law on Licensed Doctors and Drugs Control Law (Chinese-English)	6.00
17	中华人民共和国专属经济区和大陆架法、海域使用管理法(中英对照) Law on the Exclusive Economic Zone and the Continental Shelf and Law on the Administration of the Use of Sea Areas (Chinese-English)	6.00
18	中华人民共和国劳动法(中英对照) Labor Law (Chinese-English)	6.00
19	中华人民共和国招标投标法(中英对照) Bid Invitation Bidding Law (Chinese-English)	6.00
20	中华人民共和国法律汇编(民法·商法)(行政法〔经济类〕卷)(中英文) Laws of the People's Republic of China (Administrative Laws Regarding Economy and Civil Commercial Laws) (Chinese-English)	210.00
21	中华人民共和国法律汇编(1996-2001)(英文) The Laws of the People's Republic of China (1996-2001) (English)	250.00—400.00

专业化出版　个性化服务

法规中心特别推荐书目

序号	书　　　　名	定　价
1	中华人民共和国最新立法司法文告2000年第1—6辑(附光盘)	150.00
2	中华人民共和国最新立法司法文告2001年第1—6辑(附光盘)	150.00
3	中华人民共和国最新立法司法文告2002年第1—6辑(附光盘)(已出3辑)	150.00
4	公民常用法律手册(2002年版)	28.00
5	诉讼法律手册	34.00
6	赔偿法律手册	30.00
7	婚姻家庭法律手册	15.00
8	房地产法律手册	27.00
9	保险法律手册	15.00
10	金融法律手册	42.00
11	税收法律手册	21.00
12	环境保护法律手册	22.00
13	消费者权益保护法律手册	25.00
14	知识产权法律手册	25.00
15	教育法律手册	23.00
16	劳动法律手册	25.00
17	治安管理法律手册	21.00
18	交通法律手册	30.00
19	担保法律手册	20.00
20	执行法律手册	28.00
21	仲裁法律手册	27.00
22	学生常用法律手册	29.00
23	民事办案手册	29.00
24	经济办案手册(上、下)	68.00
25	刑事办案手册	32.00
26	查处经济违法犯罪政策法规手册	30.00
27	最新刑事法律及司法解释手册	31.00
28	票据纠纷案件审判手册	20.00
29	保护未成年人执法手册	29.00
30	《民事案件案由规定》释解	28.00
31	财务会计法律手册	25.00
32	法律小全书(2002年版)(附光盘)	148.00
33	证据法律手册	28.00
34	外商投资企业法律手册	28.00
35	医药卫生法律手册	28.00
36	建筑法律手册	28.00
37	商业银行法律手册	48.00
38	中华人民共和国刑法罪名适用手册	28.00
39	宪法性法律及司法解释适用手册	25.00
40	国家赔偿案件审判手册	25.00
41	中华人民共和国对外经济贸易法律法规规章新编(第一辑)	98.00
42	中华人民共和国证券期货法规汇编(2001)(附光盘)	120.00
43	中华人民共和国电子商务与网络法规汇编(修订本)	60.00
44	知识产权法律法规精选(附光盘)	78.00

专家释法　　权威读本

法律释义丛书　全国人大常委会法制工作委员会编

序号	书　　　　名	定　价
1	中华人民共和国村民委员会组织法释义	12.00
2	中华人民共和国澳门特别行政区驻军法释义	7.00
3	中华人民共和国立法法释义	20.00
4	中华人民共和国检察官法释义	16.00
5	中华人民共和国法官法释义	15.00
6	中华人民共和国引渡法释义	20.00
7	中华人民共和国工会法释义	17.00
8	中华人民共和国刑法释义	28.50
9	中华人民共和国刑法修正案释义	13.00
10	中华人民共和国刑事诉讼法释义	13.50
11	中华人民共和国预防未成年人犯罪法释义	21.00
12	全国人大常委会关于惩治骗购外汇、逃汇和非法买卖外汇犯罪的决定释义	12.00
13	中华人民共和国证券法释义	26.00
14	中华人民共和国合同法释义	38.00
15	中华人民共和国担保法释义	6.80
16	中华人民共和国信托法释义	18.00
17	中华人民共和国招标投标法释义	16.00
18	中华人民共和国个人独资企业法释义	13.00
19	中华人民共和国婚姻法释义	15.00
20	中华人民共和国著作权法释义	18.00
21	中华人民共和国商标法释义	15.00(估)
22	中华人民共和国专利法释义	14.00
23	中华人民共和国专利法实施细则释义	30.00
24	中华人民共和国国防教育法释义	10.00(估)
25	中华人民共和国动物防疫法释义	12.00
26	中华人民共和国建筑法释义	18.00
27	中华人民共和国价格法释义	14.00
28	中华人民共和国防震减灾法释义	10.60
29	中华人民共和国献血法释义	9.00
30	中华人民共和国森林法释义	15.00
31	中华人民共和国消防法释义	12.00
32	中华人民共和国土地管理法释义	22.00
33	中华人民共和国防洪法释义	14.00
34	中华人民共和国行政复议法释义	12.00
35	中华人民共和国会计法释义	20.00
36	中华人民共和国公益事业捐赠法释义	9.00
37	中华人民共和国海洋环境保护法释义	18.00
38	中华人民共和国海域使用管理法释义	11.00
39	中华人民共和国气象法释义	14.00
40	中华人民共和国税收征收管理法释义	18.00
41	中华人民共和国海关法释义	22.00
42	中华人民共和国大气污染防治法释义	20.00
43	中华人民共和国药品管理法释义	22.00
44	中华人民共和国职业病防治法释义	18.00
45	中华人民共和国产品质量法释义	23.00
46	中华人民共和国防沙治沙法释义	16.00

图书在版编目(CIP)数据

中华人民共和国公司法.—北京:法律出版社,
2002.8
(中英对照法律文本系列.12元系列)
ISBN 7-5036-2934-7

Ⅰ.中… Ⅱ. Ⅲ.公司法-中国-汉、英
Ⅳ.D922.291.91

中国版本图书馆CIP数据核字(2002)第062361号

出版/法律出版社	编辑/法规出版中心
总发行/中国法律图书公司	经销/新华书店
印刷/中国科学院印刷厂	责任印制/陶 松
开本/850×1168 1/32	印张/5 字数/110千
版本/2002年10月第1版	2002年10月第1次印刷

法律出版社地址/北京市西三环北路甲105号科原大厦A座4层(100037)
电子信箱/pholaw@public.bta.net.cn 电话/(010)88414121(总编室)
法规出版中心地址/北京市西三环北路甲105号科原大厦A座4层(100037)
电子信箱/Law@lawpress.com.cn. rpc8841@sina.com
读者热线/(010)88414136 88414113 传真/88414115
中国法律图书公司地址/北京市西三环北路甲105号科原大厦A座4层(100037)
商务网址/www.chinalaw-book.com 传真/(010)88414897
电话/(010)88414899 88414900 (021)62071679(上海公司)

出版声明/版权所有 侵权必究
书号:ISBN 7-5036-2934-7/D·2644
定价:12.00元
(如有缺页或倒装,本社负责退换)

First Edition 2002

ISBN 7 – 5036 – 2934 – 7/D·2644
Copyright 2002 by Law Press China

All rights reserved. No part of this book may be reproduced or transmitted in any form or by any means without permission in writing from the copyright owner.

Published by
Law Press China

Printed in the People's Republic of China